"…that each one may be trained under
the shadow of the protection of God,
each may become like a lighted candle
in the world of humanity,
a tender and growing plant in the rose garden of Abhá;
that these children may be so trained and educated
that they shall give life to the world of humanity;
that they may receive insight;
that they may bestow hearing upon the people of the world;
that they may sow the seeds of eternal life
and be accepted in the threshold of God…"

'Abdu'l-Bahá

COPYRIGHT NOTICE
Limited reproduction permission is granted to the purchaser of this book, to reproduce Black Line Masters, illustrations and letters to parents, as may be required for classroom use and / workshops.

© Written and Illustrated by Ruth Gordon-Smith
gsfamily19@yahoo.com
Printed – February 2006 (Second Edition)

CONTENTS PAGE

AUTHOR'S NOTES .... page 1
QUOTE VISUALISATION ACTIVITIES .... page 3
DISCUSSION METHODS .... page 5
LETTERBOX .... page 7

Term Starters
GOD .... page 15
Bahá'u'lláh .... page 23
'Abdu'l-Bahá .... page 29
THE Báb .... page 35

Virtues
ORDERLINESS .... page 43
RESPECT .... page 49
OBEDIENCE .... page 55
LOVE .... page 61
PRAYERFULNESS .... page 65
UNITY .... page 69
JUSTICE .... page 73
CONFIDENCE .... page 77
KINDNESS .... page 81
COURTESY .... page 85
CLEANLINESS .... page 91
SERVICE .... page 95
DETACHMENT .... page 101
JOYFULNESS .... page 107
THOUGHTFULNESS .... page 111
HUMILITY .... page 115
PATIENCE .... page 119
PERSEVERANCE .... page 123
RESPONSIBILITY .... page 127
TRUTHFULNESS .... page 131

Extra
SONGS / RHYMES .... page 136
GROUP FILLERS .... page 143
STAR BOX PICTURES .... page 147
BADGES .... page 149

AUTHOR'S NOTES

PURPOSE:

This program uses the Bahá'í writings to develop the virtues and noble qualities latent within all children. Children will familiarize themselves with quotations, explore the meaning of each virtue and understand the importance of their individual spiritual development and progress.

FORMAT:

Duration: A program for one year with a lesson each week.

Terms: Each term begins with two lessons on either God, Bahá'u'lláh, 'Abdu'l-Bahá, or the Báb. This is then followed by lessons based on the virtues which cover two weeks each. The order of the virtues does not matter.
Note: Prayerfulness is best done one week before Ayyam-i-Há.

CONTENT:

Star Box: A star box from the lesson on God is kept for each virtues lesson. Something different each time relating to the lesson is placed inside and the children guess what it is. The purpose is to capture the children's interest and attention. If the object needed is not easy to get, pictures are provided at the back of the book as alternatives.

Quote Visualisations: These are used to help the children become familiar with and maybe memorize the quotation. It also helps in the discussion of what the meaning is of the whole quote and also specific words. Ask the children to say each part of the quotation with you. Go over it several times. The children, by the end of the two weeks should be able say the quotation using only the pictures or even better, they will have memorized it completely. The purpose is to internalize the quotation rather than memorize although it is wonderful if they can say it by themselves. In other words, they will become familiar with the words and understand the meaning. To help memorization other activities can be implemented including covering up one picture and then another until they can say the whole thing without any pictures or words. Another game is, after they have cut the pictures out, see if the children can put them back into order from memory.

Discussions: The discussion points sheet provided allows the children to have a simple visual focus while learning what the virtue means. Other books which describe the virtues in more detail may be beneficial for the development of your own understanding before the class starts.

Stories: Each story relates to the virtue or quotation being discussed and finishes with a moral which can either be read out or discussed informally with the class.

Songs: Children usually respond well when you make up some action to teach them along with the words.

Prayers: Always ask the children to be reverent and wait for them to be sitting reverently before starting the prayer. Once children are familiar with prayer you could ask if any of them would like to say it on their own.

Games: The games are designed to give the children a more complete understanding of the virtue or quotation being discussed.

AUTHOR'S NOTES

HINTS:

Materials: Double-sided sticky tape can be used instead of glue. It can be bought from most craft shops. It can be stuck on before the lesson, does not take drying time and is very strong. Otherwise use glue sticks, Clag glue or PVA.

Crayons are often preferable to textas for young children as they cover areas more quickly and easily. They also are less likely to cover up line work such as quotations.

Shops like spotlight have craft material such as plastic eyes, magnets, etc... If specific materials like plastic eyes are not easily available they could be made out of paper, drawn on or the activity could be adapted to make it more practical.

Preparation: Depending on the size and age of the class, it may be beneficial to do some cutting and preparing of activities before class to help with lesson flow and assist those children who may take a long time to complete some tasks.

Before class make a sample of each activity so that children can see what they will be making.

It is advisable to always make an extra one or two spares for the activities in case of mistakes or extra students.

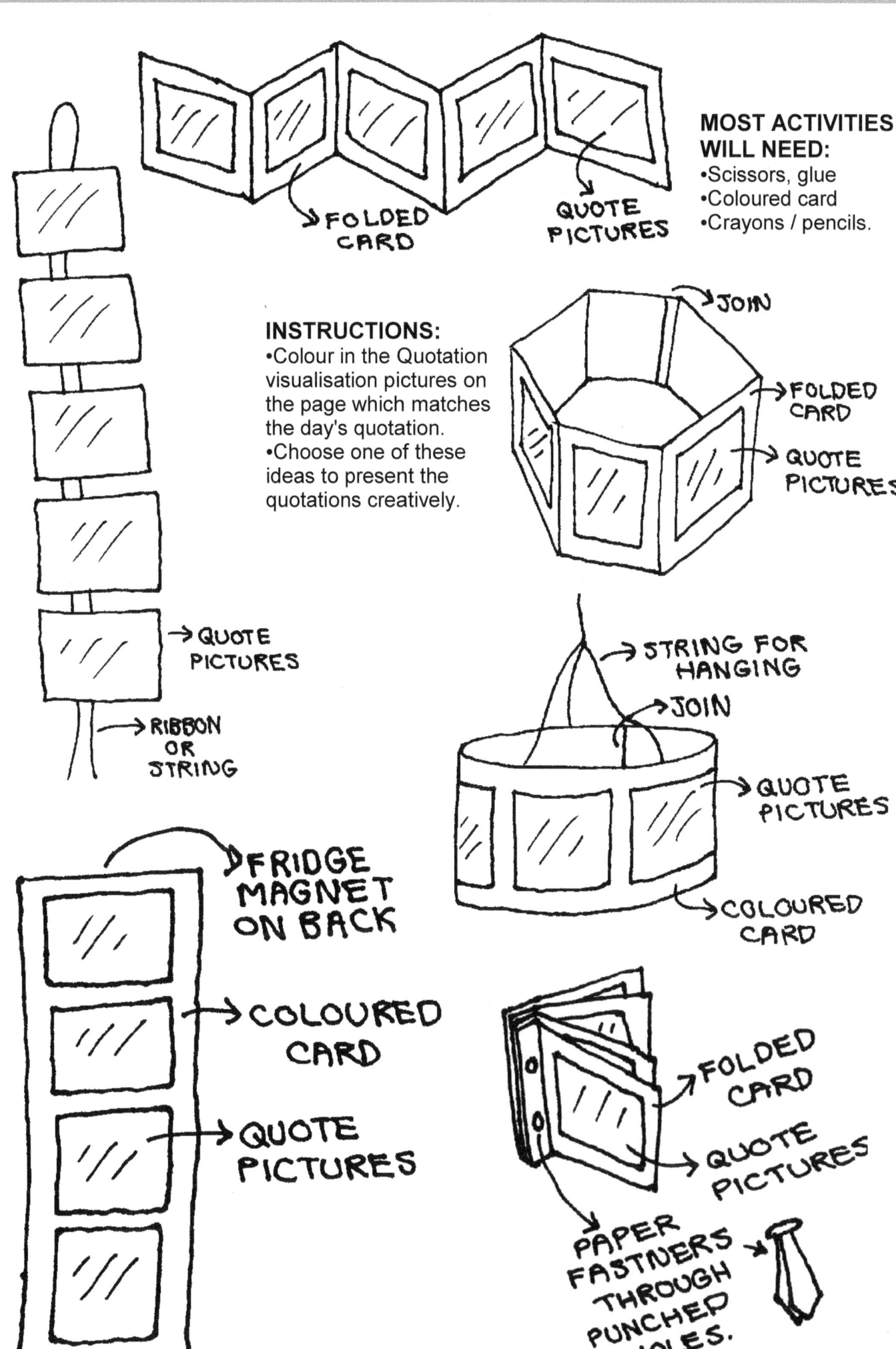

DISCUSSION POINTS

DISCUSSION FOCUS QUESTIONS - VIRTUES

- **INSTRUCTIONS:**
- Fill in the virtue of the week in the space provided.
- Discuss how the virtue can be expressed to ourselves, others, nature / environment and things.
- The ideas can be written around each picture and coloured in (optional).
- Older children can do their own (optional).

HOW CAN I BE ....(VIRTUE)
WITH MYSELF?

HOW CAN I BE ....(VIRTUE)
WITH OTHERS?

HOW CAN I BE ....(VIRTUE)
WITH THINGS?

HOW CAN I BE ....(VIRTUE)
WITH NATURE?

DISCUSSION POINTS

DISCUSSION FOCUS QUESTIONS – TERM STARTERS

- **INSTRUCTIONS:**
- Fill in the topic of the week in the space provided, eg. 'Abdu'l-Bahá.
- Discuss how they want us to treat ourselves, our friends, the world, the environment.
- The ideas can be written around each picture and coloured in (optional).
- Older children can do their own (optional).

HOW DOES ......(TOPIC)...... WANT ME TO TREAT **MYSELF?**

HOW DOES ......(TOPIC)...... WANT ME TO TREAT **MY FRIENDS?**

HOW DOES ......(TOPIC)...... WANT ME TO TREAT **THE WORLD?**

HOW DOES ......(TOPIC)...... WANT ME TO TREAT **THE ENVIRONMENT?**

LETTERBOX

LETTERBOX CONSTRUCTION

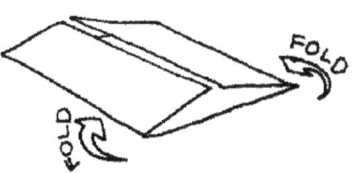
STEP 1.
Fold in each end of an A4 piece of card 7.5cm.

STEP 2.
Fold the page back up to make a U shape.

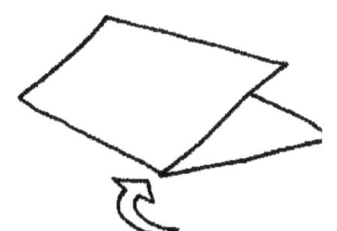
STEP 3.
Take another sheet of card. Fold it in half.

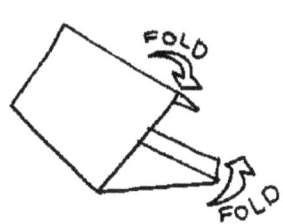
STEP 4.
Fold in each end 3.3cm

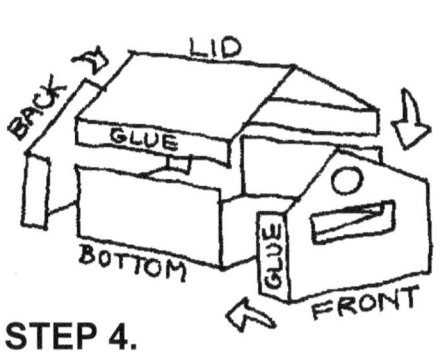
STEP 4.
Cut out the front and back.
Fold the edges in.
Glue the letter box together.

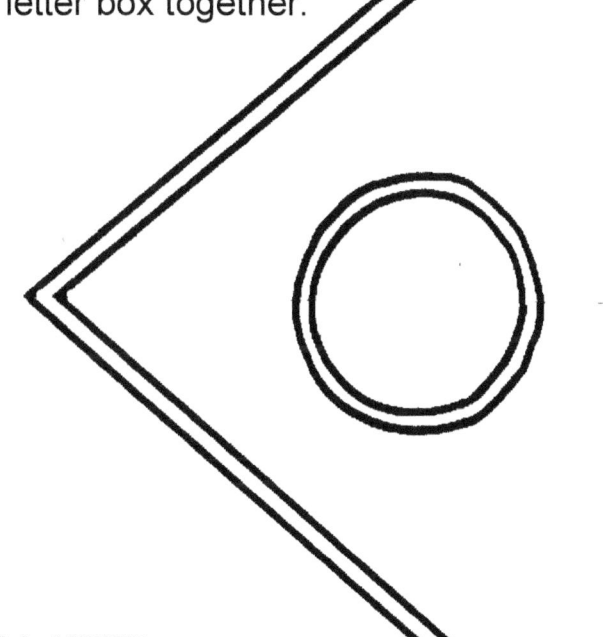

YOU WILL NEED:
- Two sheets of coloured A4 card
- This page photocopied on to A4 coloured card twice.
- Glue
- Scissors, craft knife

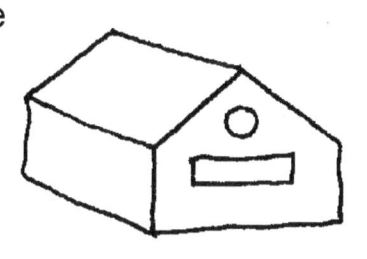

LETTERBOX

MESSAGES – FOR TERM STARTERS

"that... our faults become virtues, our ignorance transformed into knowledge; in order that we might attain the real fruits of humanity..."
— 'Abdu'l-Bahá

"Take pride not in love for yourselves but in love for your fellow-creatures. Glory not in love for your country, but in love for all mankind."
— Bahá'u'lláh

"that... each may become like a lighted candle in the world of humanity."
— 'Abdu'l-Bahá

"Purge your hearts of worldly desires, and let angelic virtues be your adorning."
— The Báb

Instructions:
- Build a letterbox using the worksheet provided.
- Cut out the quotation that is appropriate for the day.
- Place it in an envelope with the name of the class or the names of the children on the front.
- Put the letter in the box as if it has been posted.
- These are the messages the children receive at the beginning of each virtue.
- Sing the mailbox song as a child is taking the letter out of the box.

LETTERBOX

MESSAGES – FOR VIRTUES

"creation carrieth out its functions in perfect order, every separate part of it performing its own task."
— 'Abdu'l-Bahá

"that all mankind become real friends with one another and each soul respect the other."
— 'Abdu'l-Bahá

"O people be obedient to the ordinances of God"
— Bahá'u'lláh

"Make My love thy treasure and cherish it even as thy very sight and life"
— Bahá'u'lláh

"... strive that your actions day by day may be beautiful prayers."
— 'Abdu'l-Bahá

"So powerful is the light of unity that it can illuminate the whole earth."
— Bahá'u'lláh

LETTERBOX

MESSAGES – FOR VIRTUES

"Attire mine head with the crown of justice…"
— Bahá'u'lláh

"…place your whole trust and confidence in God."
— Bahá'u'lláh

"…let your heart burn with loving kindness for all who may cross your path."
— 'Abdu'l-Bahá

"O people of God!… Courtesy is… the lord of all virtues"
— Bahá'u'lláh

"As soon as the mirror is cleaned and purified, the sun will manifest itself."
— 'Abdu'l-Bahá

"Service is the magnet which attracts the heavenly strength."
— 'Abdu'l-Bahá

MESSAGES – FOR VIRTUES

LETTERBOX

"Cast away that which ye possess, and, on the wings of detachment, soar beyond all created things."
— Bahá'u'lláh

"Turn all your thoughts toward bringing joy to hearts"
— 'Abdu'l-Bahá

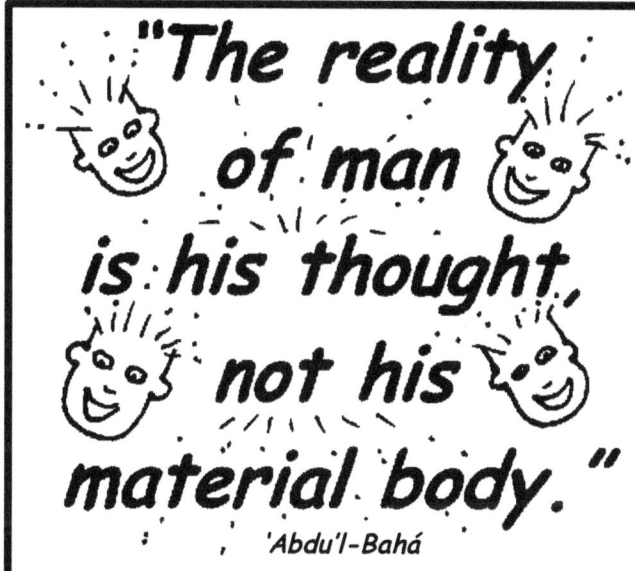

"The reality of man is his thought, not his material body."
— 'Abdu'l-Bahá

"My dominion is my humility"
— 'Abdu'l-Bahá

"Be patient under all conditions"
— Bahá'u'lláh

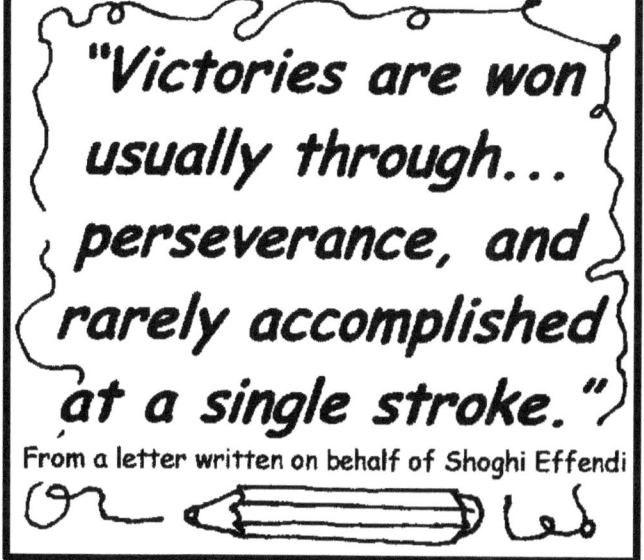

"Victories are won usually through... perseverance, and rarely accomplished at a single stroke."
From a letter written on behalf of Shoghi Effendi

LETTERBOX

MESSAGES – FOR VIRTUES

Instructions:
- Build a letterbox using the worksheet provided.
- Cut out the quotation that is appropriate for the day.
- Place it in an envelope with the name of the class or the names of the children on the front.
- Put the letter in the box as if it has been posted.
- These are the messages the children receive at the beginning of each virtue.
- Sing the mailbox song as a child is taking the letter out of the box.

TERM STARTERS

CHOOSE ONE OF THE FOLLOWING
TWO WEEK PLANS TO BEGIN
EACH NEW TERM.

LESSON PLAN

DAY 1

DISCUSSION: Who is God? Take the children outside and discuss as follows:
We cannot physically see God but we can see what he has created.
We cannot physically feel God but we can feel how much he loves us.
He cannot physically help us but he can help develop us spiritually so that we have the strength to help ourselves. He sent us special people with messages to help guide us and teach us how to live together peacefully.

PRAYER: Discuss how prayer is our way of talking to God. We can ask for assistance when we need help, thank him for the wonderful things he has already given us and ask for guidance when we feel unsure. Ask the children what they think they might like talk to God about.
"O God, Guide Me"
Use the illustrated prayer provided to discuss the meaning of the prayer.

SONG: "O God, Guide Me"
Sing with actions.

ACTIVITY:
Star Boxes – Use activity sheet provided.
Purpose – To reflect on the meaning of the prayer.

REVIEW:
Ask the children to colour in the black and white prayer so they have a copy to take home.

DAY 2

PRAYER: "O God Guide Me"
Sing with actions.

DISCUSSION REVIEW: Who is God?
Use discussion points sheet for term starters at the beginning of the book to help discuss what God wants for us and the people around us.

QUOTE:
"that... our faults become virtues, our ignorance transformed into knowledge; in order that we might attain the real fruits of humanity..."
'Abdu'l-Bahá
Place the quotation in the letterbox as described in the beginning of the book. These are the messages God has sent us through special people. Ask a child to take out the letter.
Ask the children to say the quotation with you a couple of times. Discuss what it means.

SONG: "Fruits of Humanity" - sing with actions.

STORY: "The Secret of the Apple Tree."

ACTIVITY:
Fruits of Humanity – Use activity sheet provided.
Purpose – visualize quotation – to understand that we were created to acquire divine virtues.

STAR BOXES

Instructions:
- Buy some small star boxes from a craft shop (Spotlight)
- Glue the quotation onto the bottom of the inside of the box.
- Glue shiny pieces of paper onto the box to decorate it.

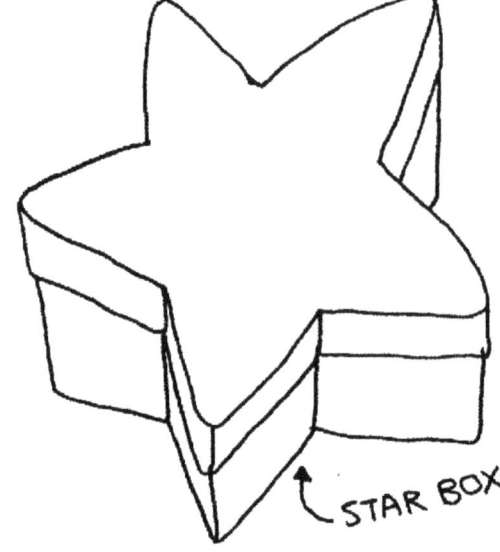

STAR BOX

Each child will need:
- Scissors
- Shiny pieces of paper
- A star box
- A quotation
- Glue

"O God... make of me... a brilliant star."
'Abdu'l-Bahá

"O God... make of me... a brilliant star."
'Abdu'l-Bahá

"O God... make of me... a brilliant star."
'Abdu'l-Bahá

"O God... make of me... a brilliant star."
'Abdu'l-Bahá

"O God... make of me... a brilliant star."
'Abdu'l-Bahá

"O God... make of me... a brilliant star."
'Abdu'l-Bahá

"O God... make of me... a brilliant star."
'Abdu'l-Bahá

"O God... make of me... a brilliant star."
'Abdu'l-Bahá

"O God... make of me... a brilliant star."
'Abdu'l-Bahá

"O God... make of me... a brilliant star."
'Abdu'l-Bahá

GOD
COLOURING IN

Instructions:
- Cut out a prayer along the dotted lines
- Cut out a piece of coloured card slightly larger than the prayer.
- Glue the prayer on to the card
- Colour in.

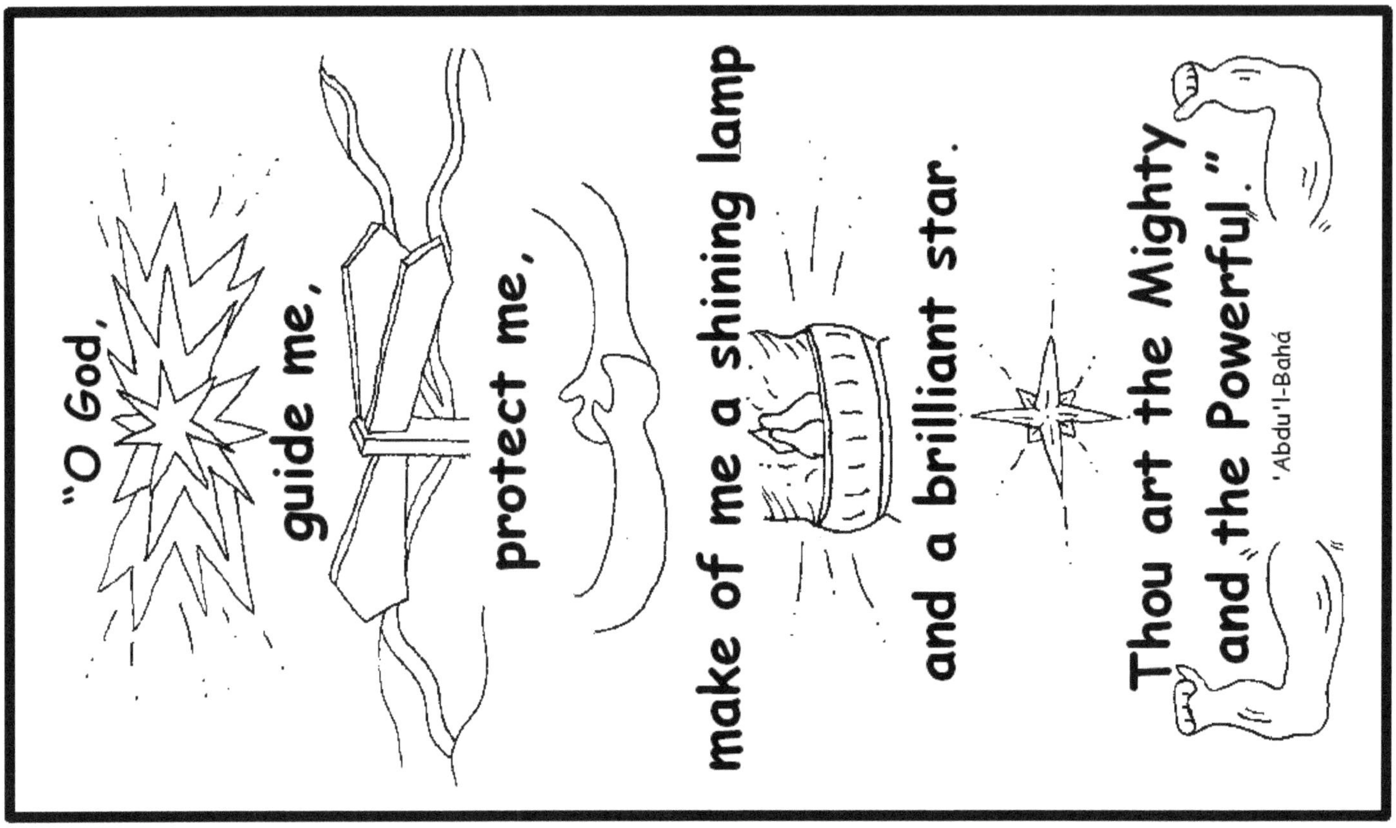

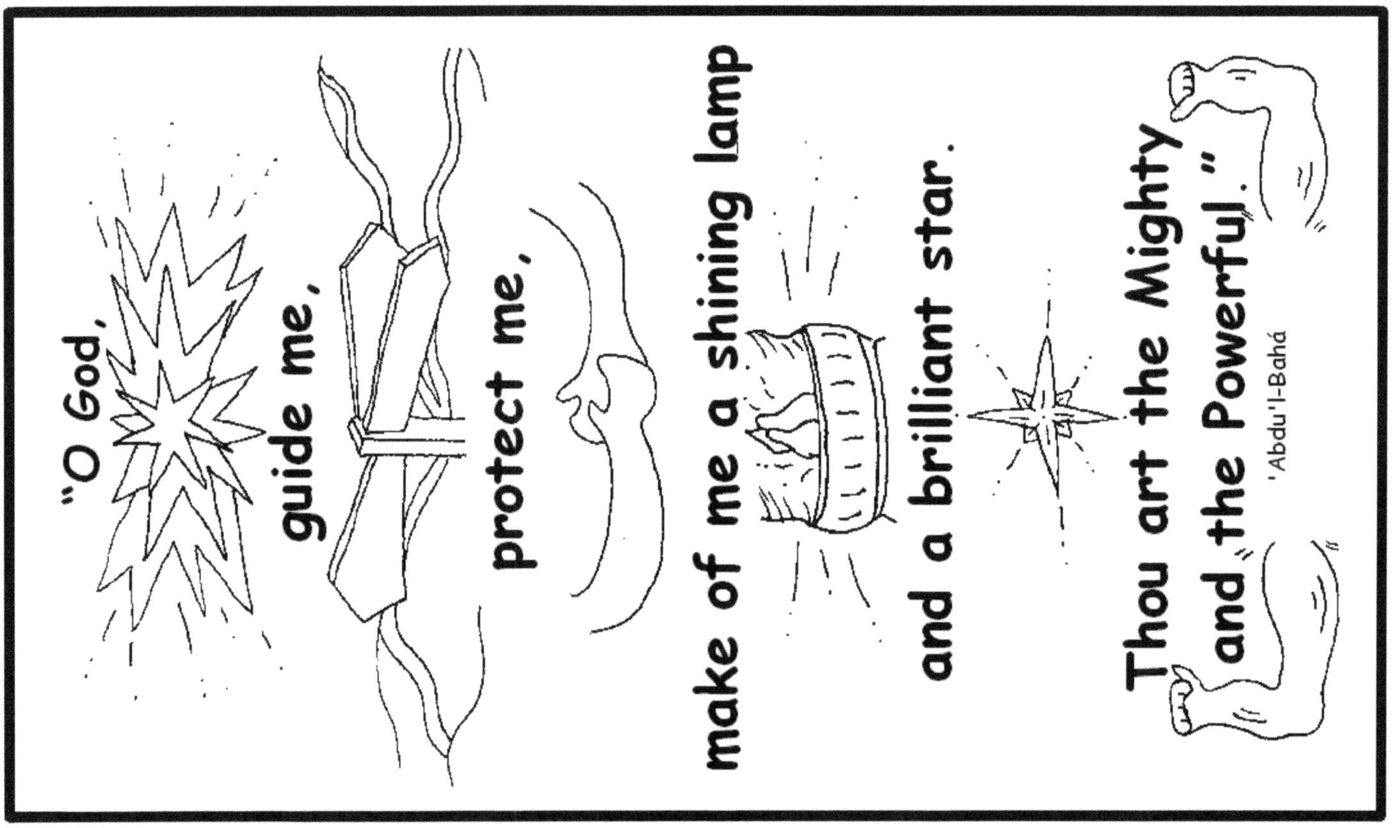

"O God, guide me, protect me, make of me a shining lamp and a brilliant star. Thou art the Mighty and the Powerful."

'Abdu'l-Bahá

"O God, guide me, protect me, make of me a shining lamp and a brilliant star. Thou art the Mighty and the Powerful."

'Abdu'l-Bahá

THE SECRET OF THE APPLE TREE

There was once a wonderful apple tree that had more fruit on it each year than any other tree in the country. People would come from far and wide just to see the amazing tree and taste its delicious fruit. People would gaze up at it and wonder why its fruit was so plentiful and each one juicier than the next.

This is the secret of the apple tree:

Each day just as the sun was coming up a little boy who loved eating apples would run all the way to the river which was a long way away and carry back a bucket of fresh water. The boy's family did not have much money and so each day he made the walk on foot with no shoes. Each time he reached the apple tree he would pour the water over the tree with love and then sit and rub his sore feet.

Then, just when the flowers were opening their petals to the sun an old lady would arrive from a nearby village, take an apple and thankfully give the tree a hug before smiling and slowly walking back home.

GOD STORY

About lunch time when everyone was indoors, a cook who worked in a restaurant near the tree would come out and kindly bury some food scraps near the roots of the tree so that the nutrients of the soil would be enriched for the tree.

Later, as the animals were scurrying back home to their nests and burrows, a man with a wooden leg would hobble past and prune the tree carefully of any dead branches so that new branches could grow. He would then take one stick with him to help him walk.

Then, finally, just as the world was getting dark and the moon coming out a young girl would appear. She would joyfully kiss the tree goodnight and leave a flower at its foot before running back home.

The tree was surrounded by love, thanks, kindness, care and joy. It received these things each day and so its leaves were green, its branches strong, its soil rich and moist and its fruit delicious. It produced for others what it was given each day.

MORAL – The virtues of humanity are like the fruit of a tree. When we feed ourselves with the knowledge of how to be loving, kind, just, friendly, co-operative and unified it will show in our actions so that we can help others attain fruits of humanity too.

GOD
FRUITS OF HUMANITY

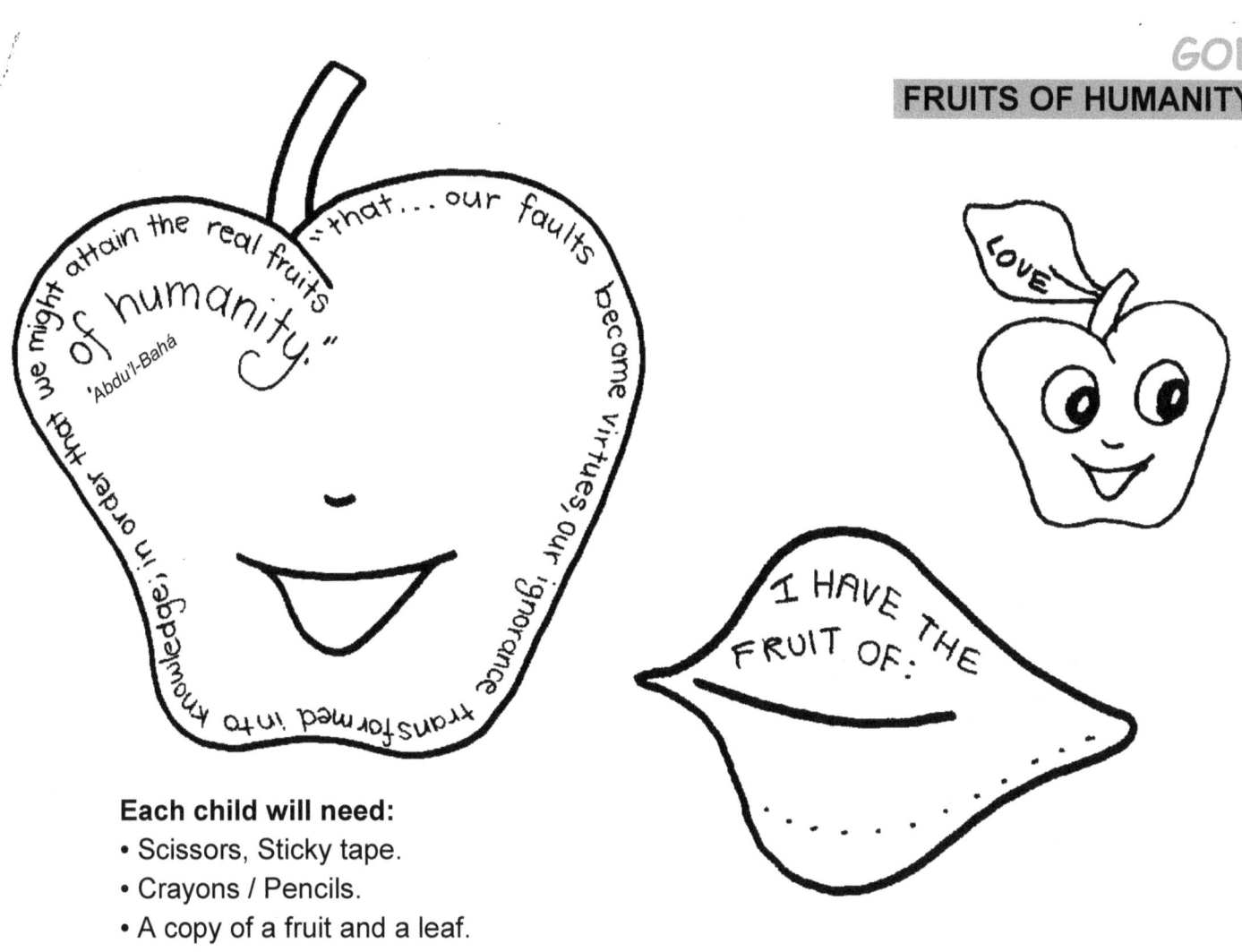

Each child will need:
- Scissors, Sticky tape.
- Crayons / Pencils.
- A copy of a fruit and a leaf.
- Two plastic eyes.
- Strong glue for eyes.
- A small stick

Instructions:
- Photocopy this page on to white card.
- Cut out a fruit and a leaf.
- Glue on two eyes.
- Colour in leaf and fruit.
- Write a virtue on the leaf.
- Tape the leaf to the fruit.
- Tape the fruit onto a small stick as if it is hanging from a tree.

BAHÁ'U'LLÁH

LESSON PLAN

DAY 1

PRAYER: Discuss how prayer is our way of talking to God. We can ask for assistance when we need help, thank him for the wonderful things he has already given us and ask for guidance when we feel unsure. Ask the children what they think they might like talk to God about.
"Blessed is the Spot"
Use the illustrated prayer provided to discuss the meaning of the prayer.

SONG: "Blessed is the Spot"
Sing with actions.

DISCUSSION: Who is Bahá'u'lláh?
He was a Messenger from God who came with a special message for the whole of humanity.
He taught us how we can be united.
He taught us that everyone is equal in the eyes of God. It doesn't matter what country they are from or what colour their hair is. Everyone is special.

ACTIVITY:
A Blessed Spot – Use activity sheet provided.
Purpose – To reflect on the meaning of the prayer.

REVIEW:
Ask the children to colour in the black and white prayer so they have a copy to take home.

DAY 2

PRAYER: "Blessed is the Spot"
Sing with actions.

DISCUSSION REVIEW: Who is Bahá'u'lláh?
Use discussion points sheet for term starters at the beginning of the book to help discuss what Bahá'u'lláh wants for us and the people around us.

QUOTE: This was Bahá'u'lláh's message to us -
"Take pride not in love for yourselves but in love for your fellow-creatures. Glory not in love for your country, but in love for all mankind."
    Bahá'u'lláh
Place the quotation in the letterbox as described in the beginning of the book. These are the messages God has sent us through special people. Ask a child to take out the letter.
Ask the children to say the quotation with you a couple of times. Discuss what it means.

SONG: "It's a Wide World" - sing with actions

STORY: "The Best"

ACTIVITY:
Mankind mobile – Use activity sheet provided.
Purpose – visualizing the quotation – to understand that Bahá'u'lláh's message embraced all mankind not just one country or one type of people and we should strive to do the same.

BAHÁ'U'LLÁH
A Blessed Spot

"Blessed is the spot... where mention of God hath been made and his praise glorified."
Bahá'u'lláh

Each child will need:
- Scissors, glue
- Magazine pictures
- A copy of this page

Instructions:
- Photocopy this page on to white card.
- Cut out the two circles.
- Cut out pictures from magazines of different places.
- Glue the pictures onto the big circle.
- Glue the quotation into the centre.

"Blessed is the spot, and the house, and the place, and the city, and the heart, and the mountain, and the refuge, and the cave, and the valley, and the land, and the sea, and the island, and the meadow where mention of God hath been made, and His praise glorified."

Bahá'u'lláh

Instructions:
- Cut out a prayer along the dotted lines
- Cut out a piece of coloured card slightly larger than the prayer.
- Glue the prayer on to the card
- Colour in.

BAHÁ'U'LLÁH
COLOURING IN

THE BEST

BAHÁ'U'LLÁH STORY

Betty was the judge for an international food festival where food was presented from all different countries around the world. The smells coming from the food made Betty's mouth water and the sight of all the beautifully prepared dishes was a sight she would never forget.

The first plate she tasted was an Italian bolognas sprinkled with fresh Parmesan cheese. "Surely there is nothing better than this," she mumbled to herself, sneaking a second mouthful.

Then she tasted a Mexican Taco which was filled with fresh salad and a very spicy sauce which Betty had to make herself stop eating or she would be too full to try any more dishes.

After that she nibbled on a shepherd's pie from England which was covered in freshly mashed potatoes and proved to be very tasty indeed.

"Goodness me," said Betty as she sampled a Chinese stir fry full of flavor and wonderful vegetables she had never seen before.

She was getting very full as she took a bite of a Danish Pastry which was so light and fluffy she could have kept eating it all day.

Finally she munched on a Hamburger from America which was flavorsome beyond belief.

"Mm, yum, yum," cried Betty as she finished her round. She thought about it for the rest of the morning, trying to decide which one she loved best. Finally she stood up on the platform to announce the winner.

Betty said "They are all very tasty and I could not decide between them so I would like to award everyone as the best. I could not love one country any better than another. So the winner is the world. They are all the best."

MORAL – We should love everyone not just the people who are the same as us, or who live near us.

BAHÁ'U'LLÁH
Mankind Mobile

--- cut

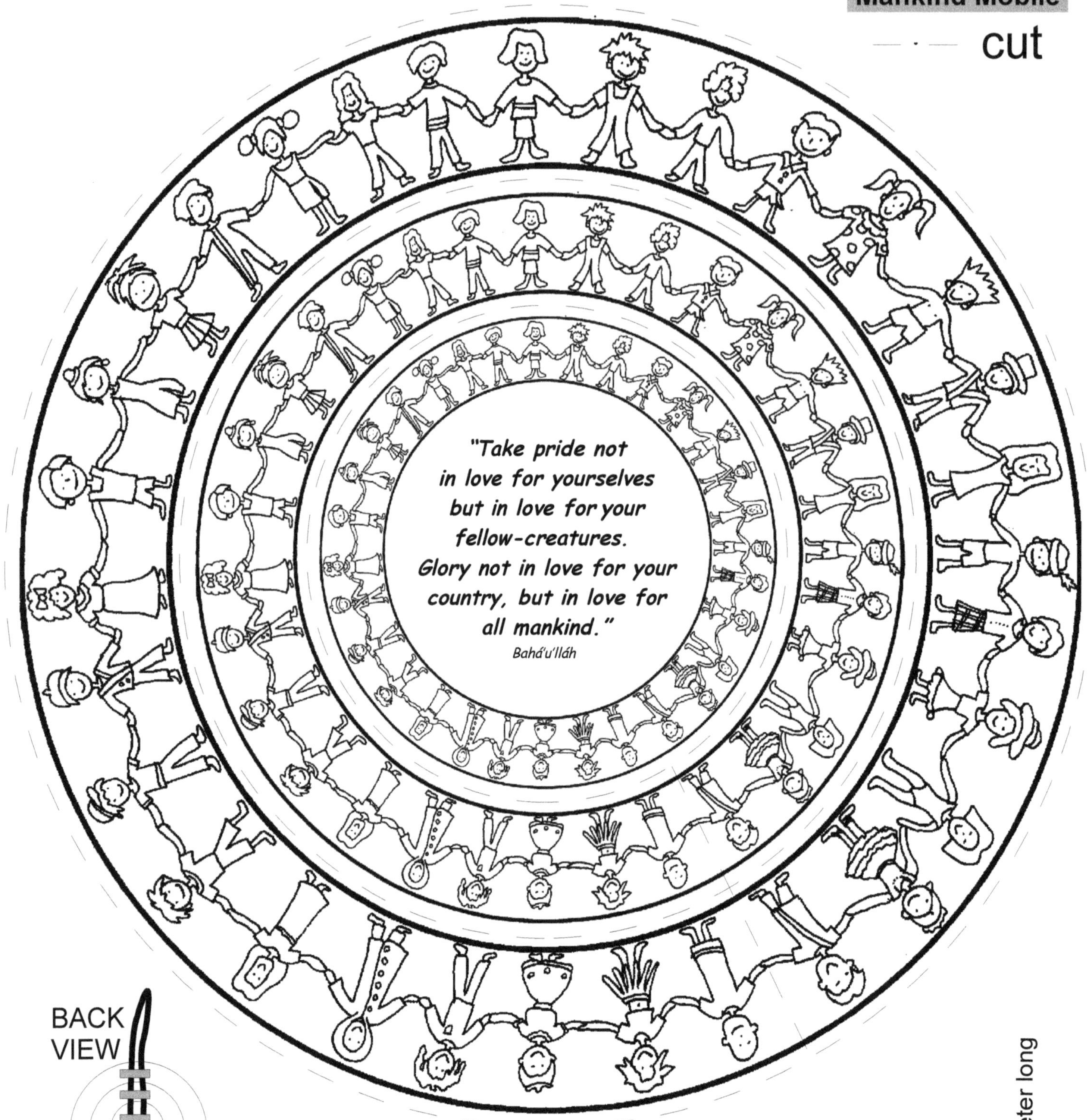

"Take pride not in love for yourselves but in love for your fellow-creatures. Glory not in love for your country, but in love for all mankind."
Bahá'u'lláh

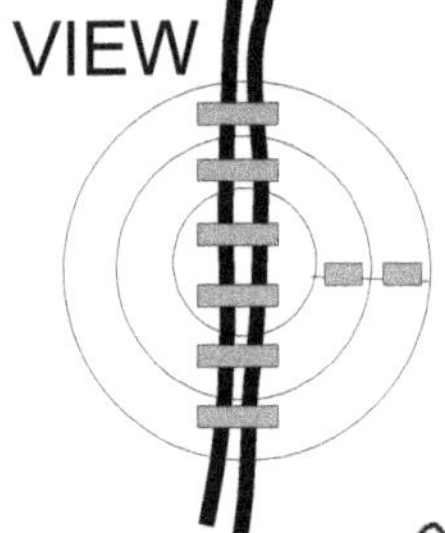

BACK VIEW

Instructions:
- Photocopy this page on to white card.
- Cut out the three circles
- Tape each circle together again on the back where it was cut to get through to the next circle.
- Colour in
- Turn the circles onto the table face down with each of the circles sitting neatly inside each other.
- Tape a piece of string onto the back of each circle so that it makes a loop at the top.
- Turn the circle at angles ready for hanging.

Each child will need:
- Sticky tape, Scissors
- Crayons / pencils
- A copy of this page
- A piece of string approximately 1 meter long

28

'ABDU'L-BAHÁ

LESSON PLAN

DAY 1

PRAYER: Discuss how prayer is our way of talking to God. We can ask for assistance when we need help, thank him for the wonderful things he has already given us and ask for guidance when we feel unsure. Ask the children what they think they might like talk to God about.
"O God! Educate these Children"
Use the illustrated prayer provided to discuss the meaning of the prayer.

SONG: "O God! Educate these Children"
Sing with actions.

DISCUSSION: Who is 'Abdu'l-Bahá?
'Abdu'l-Bahá was the son of Bahá'u'lláh. He was our example of how we should act and think. He was a very kind and generous person. He cared for sick people and helped people who had no money. He loved to see people happy - show a photograph.

ACTIVITY:
Notebook – Use activity sheet provided.
Purpose – To reflect on the meaning of the prayer.

REVIEW:
Ask the children to colour in the black and white prayer so they have a copy to take home.

DAY 2

PRAYER: "O God! Educate these Children"
Sing with actions.

DISCUSSION REVIEW: Who is 'Abdu'l-Bahá?
Use discussion points sheet for term starters at the beginning of the book to help discuss what 'Abdu'l-Bahá wants for us and the people around us.

QUOTE: This was 'Abdu'l-Bahá's message to us -
"that... each may become like a lighted candle in the world of humanity."
    'Abdu'l-Bahá
Place the quotation in the letterbox as described in the beginning of the book. These are the messages God has sent us through special people. Ask a child to take out the letter.
Ask the children to say the quotation with you a couple of times. Discuss what it means.

SONG: "Be A Candle" - sing with actions.

STORY: "Colin Candle"

ACTIVITY:
People Candles – Use activity sheet provided.
Purpose – visualizing the quotation – to understand that 'Abdu'l-Bahá wanted us to become someone who others are attracted to by our good actions, words and behaviour.

'ABDU'L-BAHÁ
NOTEBOOK

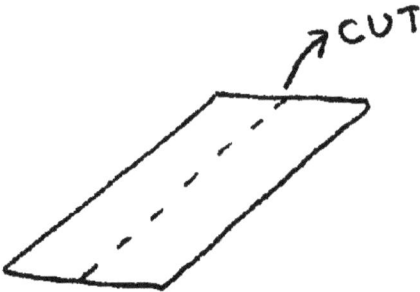

STEP 1.
Cut three A4 pages in half lengthwise for each child.

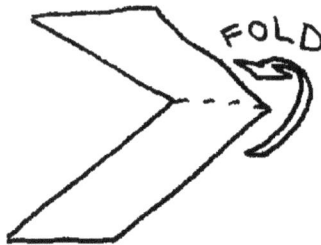

STEP 2.
Fold pages in half.

STEP 3.
Repeat steps one and two with a coloured sheet. Tie them together with wool or ribbon to make a book. Glue quotation on to front.

EACH CHILD WILL NEED:
- Half a sheet of coloured A4 card
- Three sheets of white A4 paper
- Scissors, glue
- A piece of ribbon or wool

"O God! Educate these Children"
'Abdu'l-Bahá

"O God! Educate these Children"
'Abdu'l-Bahá

'ABDU'L-BAHÁ
COLOURING IN

Instructions:
- Cut out a prayer along the dotted lines
- Cut out a piece of coloured card slightly larger than the prayer.
- Glue the prayer on to the card
- Colour in.

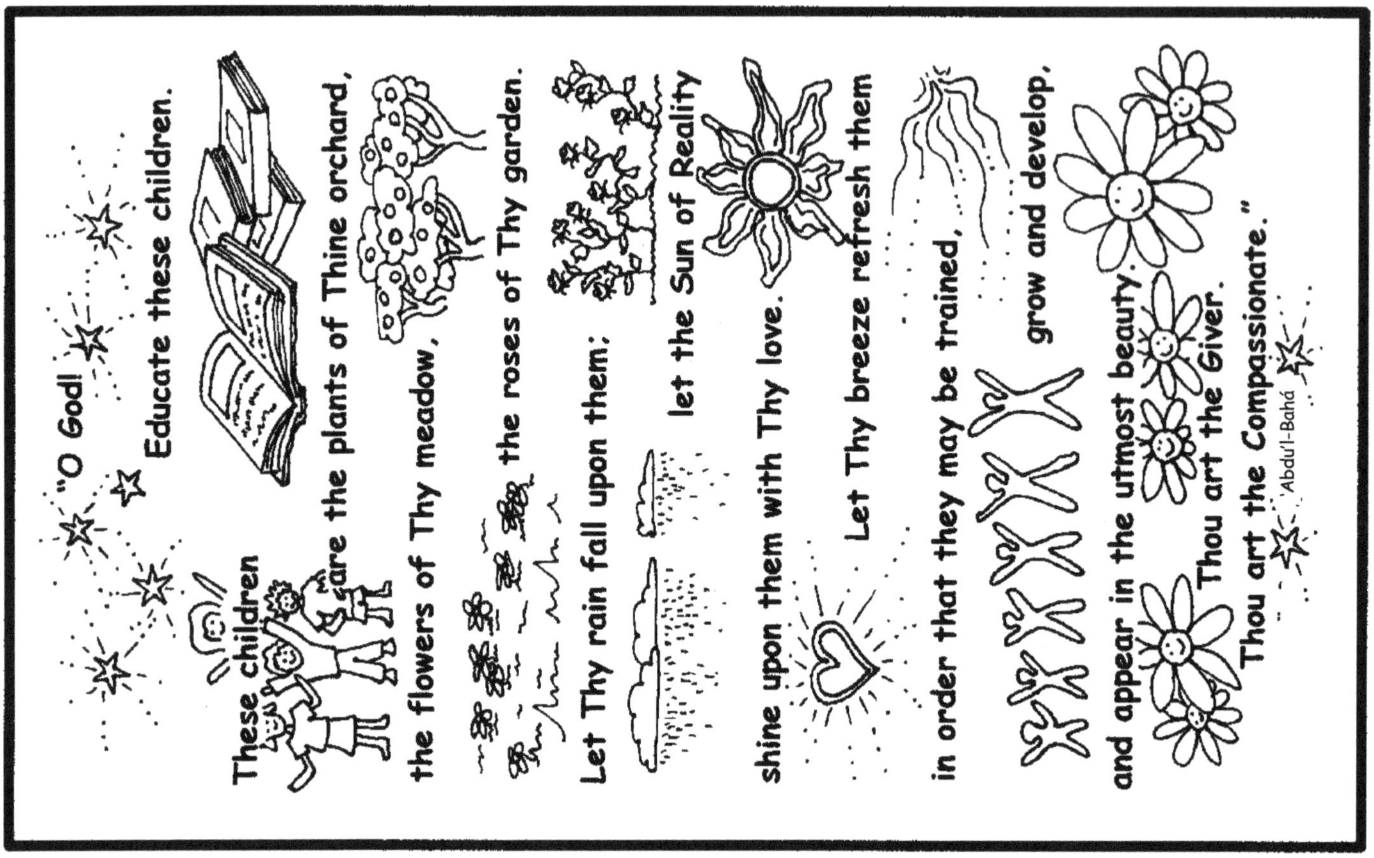

"O God! Educate these children. These children are the plants of Thine orchard, the flowers of Thy meadow, the roses of Thy garden. Let Thy rain fall upon them; let the Sun of Reality shine upon them with Thy love. Let Thy breeze refresh them in order that they may be trained, grow and develop, and appear in the utmost beauty. Thou art the Giver. Thou art the Compassionate."

—'Abdu'l-Bahá

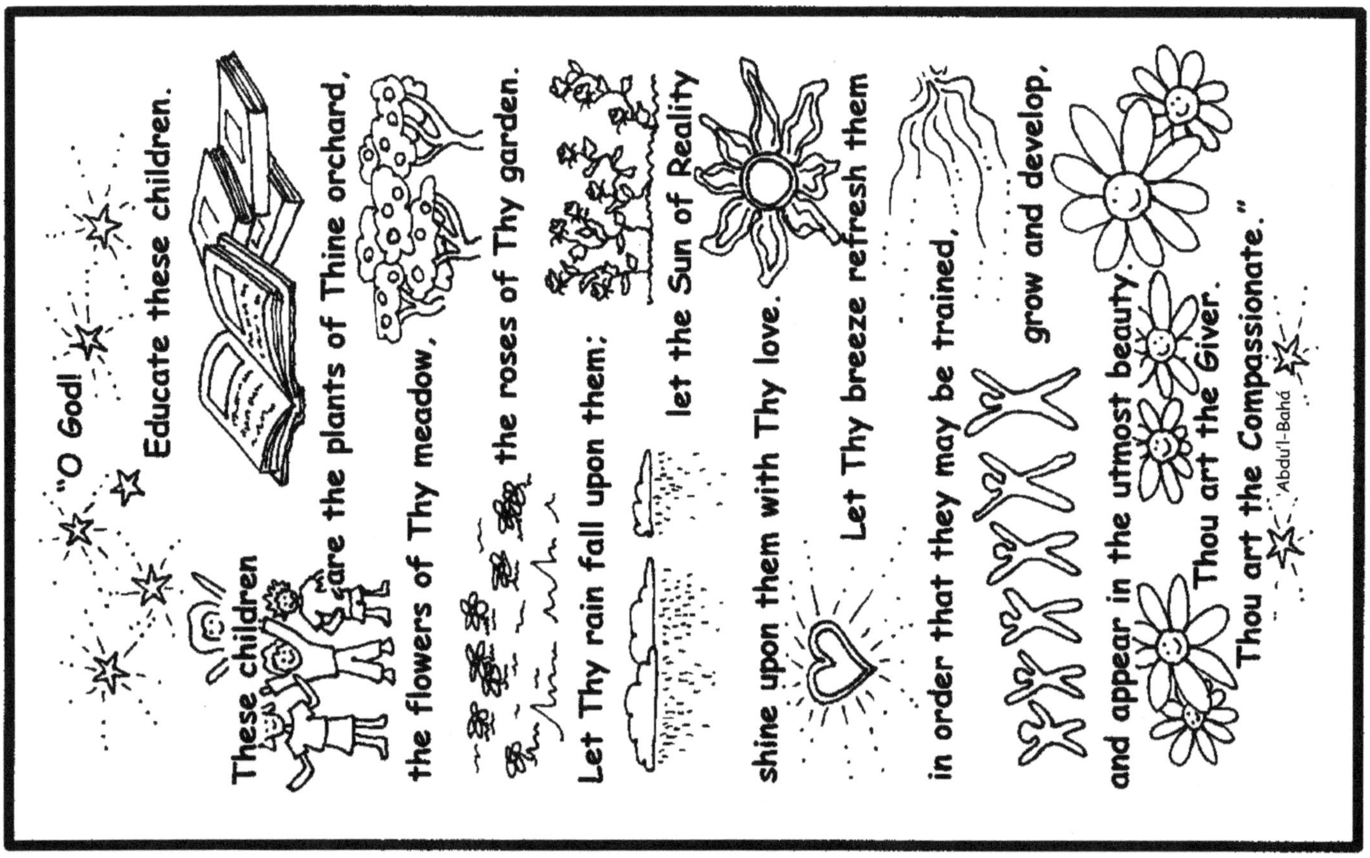

COLIN CANDLE

'ABDU'L-BAHÁ
STORY

Colin was a candle who when lit would drip wax on everything and then his flame would go out again with a big poof. Colin was depressed and grumpy and miserable. He never had anything nice to say and complained about everything. "The light's too bright," he would moan when the morning sun came in. Then, when it became dark he would groan and say "It's too dark, I can't see anything."

The other candles who were always quite happy would bob their the heads and wave their flames about letting the light flicker all over the room. "Stop being so gloomy," exclaimed Marcy, a short stumpy candle. "Your getting me down."
"There's nothing to be happy about," whined Colin Candle again.
"Oh, stop it," said Francis with a sigh.
"It's hard to be happy when your being so sad."
"Your making us feel down and then all our lights will go out," stated Frank the candle who was always making statements about something.
"We are going to be in the dark," wailed Lucy who was starting to sob. Colin candle looked at them all. "Do I really effect you that much," he queried.
"Yes," all the candles said at the same time.
"Well, I can't do anything about it" said Colin.

That night all the candles were lit but as it got dark the candles started to drip their wax sadly and one by one all their flames went poof and went out. The room got darker and darker until the only light remaining was Colin candle who's flame didn't go out because for once he wasn't thinking of himself. Instead he was looking on in astonishment as all the candles got sadder and sadder. Well, he thought, this just isn't right. He gave it some thought and smiling brighter than he had ever done before, he started hopping about. He went first to one candle and then to another and as he hopped his flame lit the other candles again. By the time Colin candle had finished the room was flickering with brilliant candle light, but the brightest of all was Colin candle who was smiling grandly, proudly waving his flame about.

MORAL – We affect others around us when we are happy and when we are sad. We should be like a candle that gives off light and makes everything around us a brighter and happier place.

'ABDU'L-BAHÁ
PEOPLE CANDLES

Instructions:
- Photocopy this page on to white card.
- Cut out a person.
- Colour in.
- Tape a matchstick to the back of the head.
- Tape a piece of cellophane to the matchstick so that it looks like a flame.
- Tape a small piece of paper on either end to the back so that it can sit around a finger as a finger puppet.

Each child will need:
- Sticky tape, Scissors
- Crayons / pencils
- A copy of a person
- A matchstick
- A piece of red or orange cellophane
- A small piece of paper about 3cm by 1cm.

STICKY TAPE

BACK   FRONT

"that... each may become like a lighted candle in the world of humanity."
— 'Abdu'l-Bahá

"that... each may become like a lighted candle in the world of humanity."
— 'Abdu'l-Bahá

"that... each may become like a lighted candle in the world of humanity."
— 'Abdu'l-Bahá

"that... each may become like a lighted candle in the world of humanity."
— Abdu'l-Bahá

LESSON PLAN

DAY 1

PRAYER: Discuss how prayer is our way of talking to God. We can ask for assistance when we need help, thank him for the wonderful things he has already given us and ask for guidance when we feel unsure. Ask the children what they think they might like to talk to God about.
"O God, My God, my Beloved, My heart's Desire!"
Use the illustrated prayer provided to discuss the meaning of the prayer.

SONG: "O God, My God, my Beloved, My heart's Desire!"
Sing with actions.

DISCUSSION: Who is the Báb?
The Báb was the gate, the herald of the cause, he prepared people for the coming of Bahá'u'lláh.
The Báb was another messenger who came from God.

ACTIVITY:
My Heart – Use activity sheet provided.
Purpose – To reflect on the meaning of the prayer.

REVIEW:
Ask the children to colour in the black and white prayer so they have a copy to take home.

DAY 2

PRAYER: "O God, My God, my Beloved, My heart's Desire!"
Sing with actions.

DISCUSSION REVIEW: Who is the Báb?
Use discussion points sheet for term starters at the beginning of the book to help discuss what the Báb wants for us and the people around us.

QUOTE: This was the Báb's message to us -
"Purge your hearts of worldly desires, and let angelic virtues be your adorning."
The Báb
Place the quotation in the letterbox as described in the beginning of the book. These are the messages God has sent us through special people. Ask a child to take out the letter.
Ask the children to say the quotation with you a couple of times. Discuss what it means.

SONG: "Getting Dressed" - sing with actions

STORY: "Choices"

ACTIVITY:
Virtues necklace – Use activity sheet provided.
Purpose – to visualise the quotation.

THE BÁB
MY HEART

"O God, My God, my Beloved, My heart's Desire!"
The Báb

Instructions:
- Photocopy this page on to white card.
- Cut out a large heart and a small heart.
- Glue shiny pieces of paper around the outside of the big heart.
- Trim the edges
- Glue the small heart on to the big heart.
- Tape a piece of wool on to the back of the heart for hanging or using as a necklace.

"O God, My God, my Beloved, My heart's Desire!"
The Báb

Each child will need:
- Sticky tape, scissors, glue
- A copy of a big heart and a small heart.
- Pieces of shiny paper.
- A piece of wool, ribbon or string.

"O God,  My God, 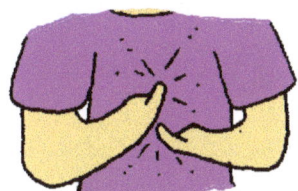 my Beloved, 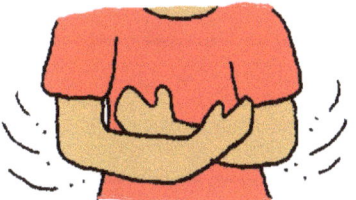 My heart's Desire!"

The Báb

THE BÁB
COLOURING IN

Instructions:
- Cut out a prayer along the dotted lines
- Cut out a piece of coloured card slightly larger than the prayer.
- Glue the prayer on to the card
- Colour in.

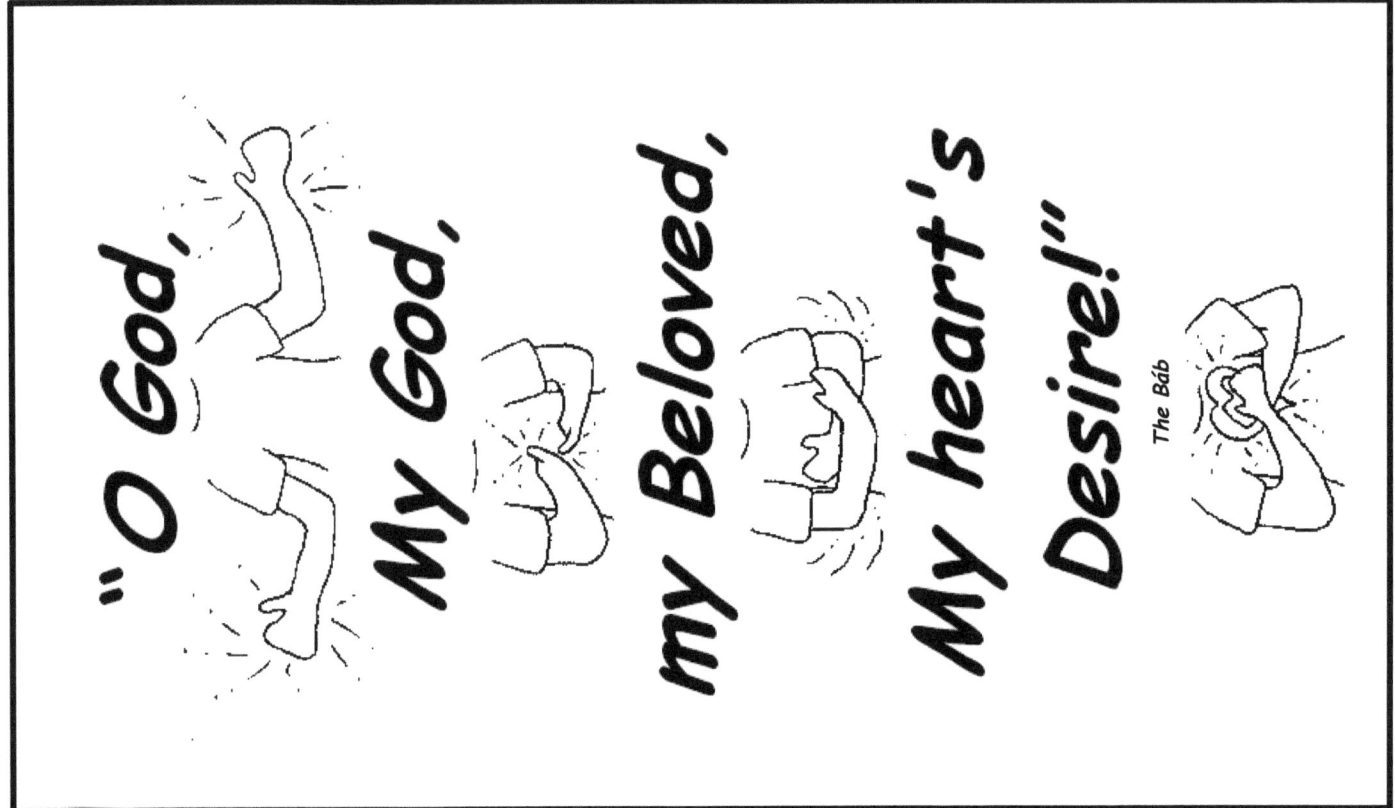

"O God, My God, my Beloved, My heart's Desire!"
— The Báb

"O God, My God, my Beloved, My heart's Desire!"
— The Báb

CHOICES

THE BÁB
STORY

Lance was playing a game of treasure hunt with Ronald. They had to follow the clues to find the treasure. Ronald was not as old as Lance and so Lance always got to the clues first.

The first clue said that they had to find the tallest tree in the garden. Ronald got there first and with it he found two lollies. He went to put them into his pocket before Ronald saw them but then he thought, "no, that wasn't right". He turned around and gave Ronald one of the lollies and read out the next clue. "Go to the back door" it said.

The boys ran off and just when Lance was about to get their first again he thought, "no that's not right," and instead he slowed down and pretended to be tired so that Ronald could find the clue first this time. The next clue read "Go to the pile of dirt."

The boys ran off and Lance picked up the clue. He read the clue quietly to himself. "Go to the flower bush to find the treasure." Lance opened his mouth to tell Ronald that the treasure was somewhere else so that he could have it all to himself but then he thought, "that is just not right", so he told him the truth instead.

They both ran off together and found under the flower bush a little box with lollies in it and a note saying, "Congratulations, you found the treasure."

Ronald couldn't count and Lance was very tempted to count them out so it looked like they had the same amount but really he had more. Then he thought, "that just isn't right". So, he counted them out so they both had exactly the same amount. Then they sat down together and ate happily while they chatted about what fun the treasure hunt was.

MORAL - We can choose how we want to be as people. Choosing to be kind and generous makes us and everyone else around us happier even when it sometimes means giving something up.

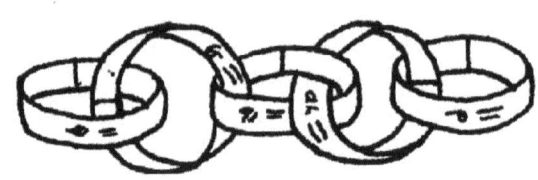

THE BÁB
Virtues Necklace

Love

Kindness

Friendliness

Truthfulness

Generosity

Gentleness

Creativity

Perseverance

Detachment

Service

Unity

INSTRUCTIONS:
- Cut out the virtues strips
- Colour each strip a different colour.
- Glue them together to make a necklace

EACH CHILD WILL NEED:
- Glue
- Scissors
- A photocopy of this sheet on to White card.
- Crayons / Pencils

VIRTUES

CHOOSE THE VIRTUES IN
ANY ORDER
Note: Prayerfulness should be
done a week before Ayyam-i-Há.

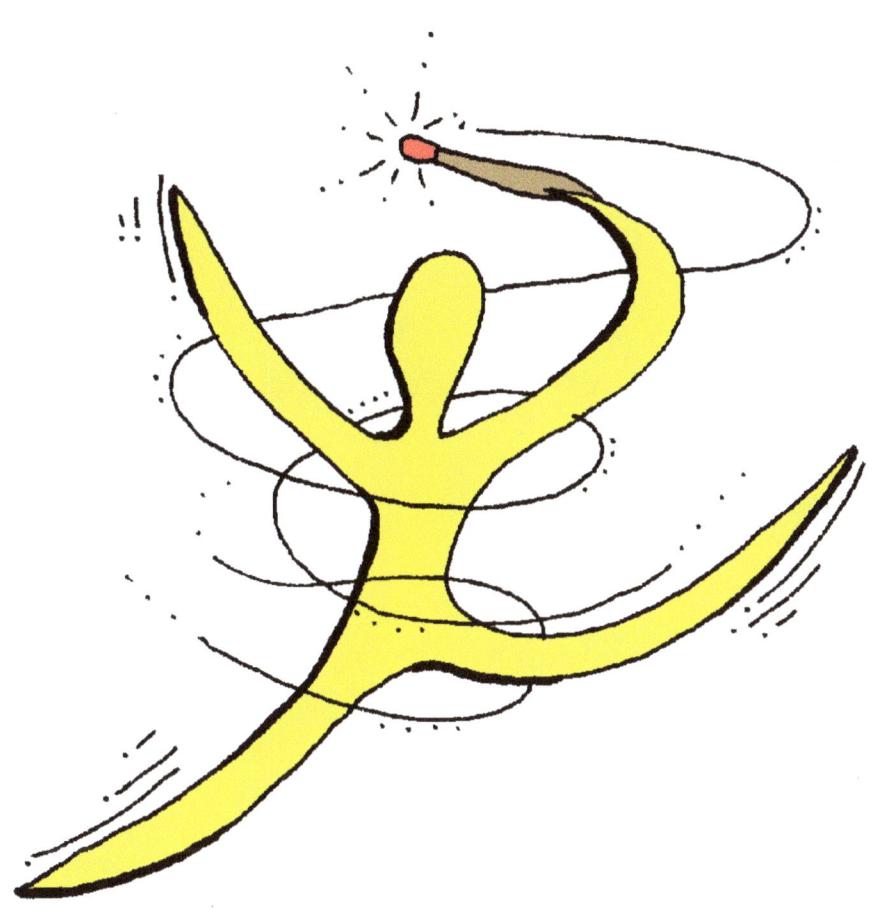

ORDERLINESS

LESSON PLAN

DAY 1

PRAYER: Sing prayers that have been learnt and any others that the children know. Ask them to be reverent because they are talking to God.

STAR BOX: What is in the box? Some toys (relate it to the story)

STORY: "I'm lost in my bedroom"

DISCUSSION: What does orderliness mean?
What does it mean to make your bedroom orderly?
If your room is a mess and you kind find what you are looking for what should you do?
Optional - Use discussion points sheet at the beginning of the book to help discuss the meaning of orderliness.

SONG: "Clean It Up" - sing with actions.

QUOTE:
"creation carrieth out its functions in perfect order, every separate part of it performing its own task ."
    'Abdu'l-Bahá

Place the quotation in the letterbox as described in the beginning of the book. These are the messages God has sent us through special people. Ask a child to take out the letter.
Ask the children to say the quotation with you a couple of times. Discuss what it means.

Discussion - Everything in creation has a special place or job and it is because of this order that everything can live together in harmony. It is the same with things like our bedroom. If we don't put things away in their special place then we have chaos. We won't be able to find things and things can get broken. Being orderly gives our lives harmony.

ACTIVITY: Orderly jigsaw – Use activity sheet on the next page. Get them to draw and colour a picture of creation (examples: a garden, planets, people, a forest).
Purpose – visualizing the quotation – how each piece in creation has a part to play like the pieces of a puzzle.

DAY 2

PRAYER: Sing prayers that have been learnt and any others that the children know. Ask them to be reverent because they are talking to God.

SONG: "Clean It Up" - sing with actions.

DISCUSSION REVIEW: What does orderliness mean?

GAME: Ask the children to swap jigsaws and see if they can do each others or give out some new ones.
Purpose – to see how the pieces mean nothing by themselves but when they are put together in the right order they make a beautiful picture.

QUOTE VISUALISATION:
*"creation carrieth out its functions in perfect order, every separate part
of it performing its own task ."*
    'Abdu'l-Bahá

Photocopy the quote visualisation page. Go through the quote with the children to help them become familiar with the words and understand the meaning. Older children may be able to memorize it. Give each child a copy of the page to colour in. Choose an activity from the front of the book to present the quotations creatively.

INSTRUCTIONS: Place the jigsaw in an envelope or bag so that the pieces don't get lost.
• Photocopy this sheet on to a piece of A4 white card. Cut along the dotted lines with a craft knife.
• Glue the border of the jigsaw on to the centre of a sheet of A4 coloured card.
• Ask the children to draw a picture of nature on the loose piece of white card. Cut into about 8 pieces.
EACH CHILD WILL NEED: Scissors, craft knife (for adult use only), crayons, pencils, glue, one piece of white card and one piece of coloured card.

ORDERLINESS
ORDERLY JIGSAWS

"creation carrieth out its functions in perfect order, every separate part of it performing its own task". 'Abdu'l-Bahá

Quote Visualisation

ORDERLINESS

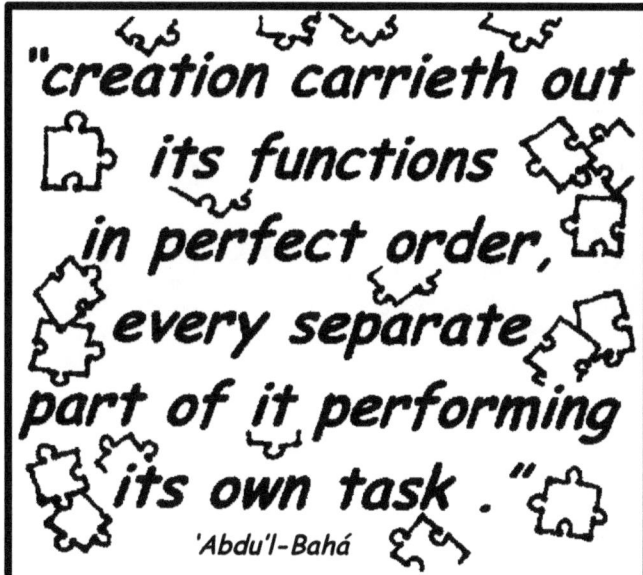

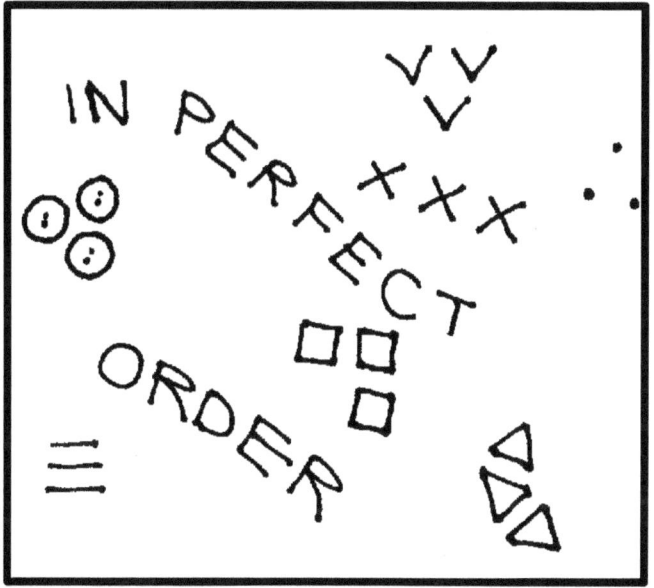

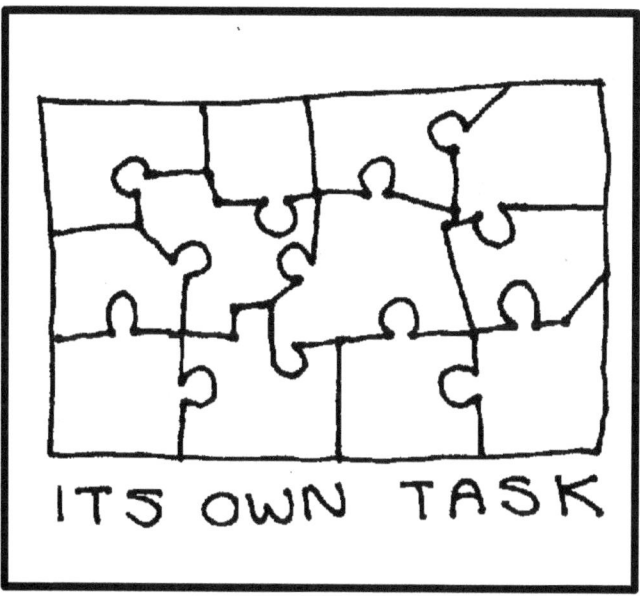

ORDERLINESS
STORY

I'M LOST IN MY BEDROOM

"Clean your room," said mum

"I will in a minute," said Curly and she kept playing with her blocks.

A few minutes later mum said, "Clean your room"

"I will, I will," replied Curly but instead of putting away her cars she pulled out more.

"Make sure your room is clean before dinner," called mum again.

"Yes, Yes," said Curly as she set up a cubby in the middle of the room.

"10 minutes to dinner," said mum.

"ALRIGHT," said Curly setting up a teddy bears' picnic in the cubby house.

"5 minutes," said mum

"Ok, Ok," yelled Curly who was hanging stars and moons from the ceiling.

ORDERLINESS
STORY

"DINNER," called mum

"Mum, Mum, I'm lost in my bedroom," screamed Curly.

"You will have to create some order in here," exclaimed mum, poking her head through the door, "or no-one will ever find you".

"I think your right," moaned Curly as she packed away her blocks.

"Oh dear," said Curly as she put away her cars.

"Goodness," exclaimed Curly as she pulled down the tent.

"Oops," Curly thought as she dismantled the teddy bear's picnic.

"Wow," said Curly as she took down the stars and moons from the ceiling.

"That's better," said Curly as she found the door and walked out ready for dinner.

"Everything in order," asked mum.

"Yes, Yes," replied Curly with a big smile on her face.

MORAL - Orderliness means keeping things tidy so that we can do all the things we want to do.

RESPECT

LESSON PLAN

DAY 1

PRAYER: Sing prayers that have been learnt and any others that the children know. Ask them to be reverent because they are talking to God.

STAR BOX: What is in the box? Friendship chain - chain of paper men (relate it to the story)

STORY: "A Friend Like Me"

DISCUSSION: What does respect mean?
Who can you show respect to?
If you are being respectful to someone, how does it make them feel?
Optional - Use discussion points sheet at the beginning of the book to help discuss the meaning of respect.

SONG: "Respect" - sing with actions.

QUOTE:

"that ... all mankind become real friends with one another and each soul respect the other."
'Abdu'l-Bahá

Place the quotation in the letterbox as described in the beginning of the book. These are the messages God has sent us through special people. Ask a child to take out the letter.
Ask the children to say the quotation with you a couple of times. Discuss what it means.

Discussion – Mankind is made up of many different people and sometimes it is easy to focus on how different we are instead of the things that bind us together. Respect allows us to see each person as a real friend and look at the differences between us as things that make the world more interesting and wonderful rather than as things that separate us and divide us.

ACTIVITY: Flower of respect – Use activity sheets on the next 2 pages.
Purpose – to visualize quotation – showing how we need to all strive to be real friends with each other by respecting each other.

DAY 2

PRAYER: Sing prayers that have been learnt and any others that the children know. Ask them to be reverent because they are talking to God.

SONG: "Respect" - sing with actions.

DISCUSSION REVIEW: What does respect mean?

GAME: Divide the group into pairs. One person talks about something that makes them very happy or very sad. The other person shows respect by sitting and listening. Then swap over and the other person talks.
Purpose - to practice being respectful.

QUOTE VISUALISATION:

"that ... all mankind become real friends with one another and each soul respect the other."
'Abdu'l-Bahá

Photocopy the quote visualisation page. Go through the quote with the children to help them become familiar with the words and understand the meaning. Older children may be able to memorize it. Give each child a copy of the page to colour in. Choose an activity from the front of the book to present the quotations creatively.

RESPECT
FLOWER OF RESPECT

EACH CHILD WILL NEED:
- One sheet of yellow A4 paper
- One sheet of green A4 paper
- A quotation circle copied on to blue paper
- Scissors, sticky tape, glue
- One long pipecleaner
- A copy of the three templates on card.
- Crayons / pencils
- Stapler

TEMPLATE B

TEMPLATE A

TEMPLATE C

STEP 1.
Fold a yellow A4 page in half lengthwise

STEP 2.
Fold in half again

STEP 3.
Fold in half diagonally

STEP 4.
Cut out template A and draw around it, then cut along outline.

STEP 5.
Repeat steps 1 to 3 with a sheet of green A4 paper. Cut out templates B and C. Place template B on to the top end of the folded paper and template B into the corner. Trace around the templates.

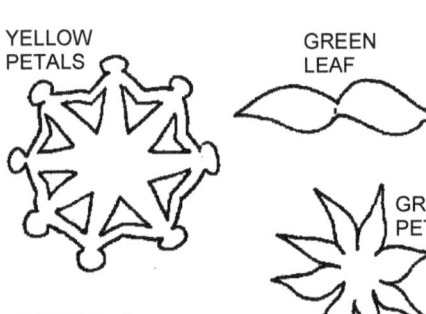

STEP 6.
Unfold and colour / decorate all three parts of the flower.

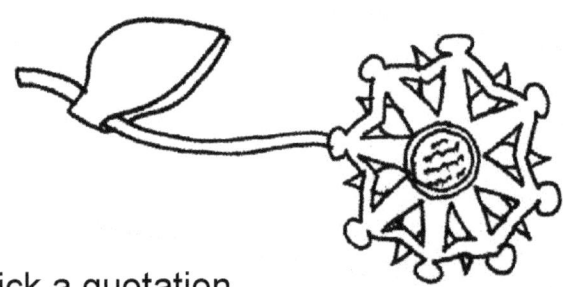

STEP 7.
Cut and stick a quotation circle on to the front of the yellow petals and stick the green petals on to the back (curl them slightly.) Staple a quotation circle from the next page on to the front of the flower. Stick the leaf on to a pipe cleaner and then tape or staple the pipe cleaner on to the back of the flower for a stem.

RESPECT
FLOWER OF RESPECT

"THAT... ALL MANKIND BECOME REAL FRIENDS WITH ONE ANOTHER AND EACH SOUL RESPECT THE OTHER."
'Abdu'l-Bahá

RESPECT

Quote Visualisation

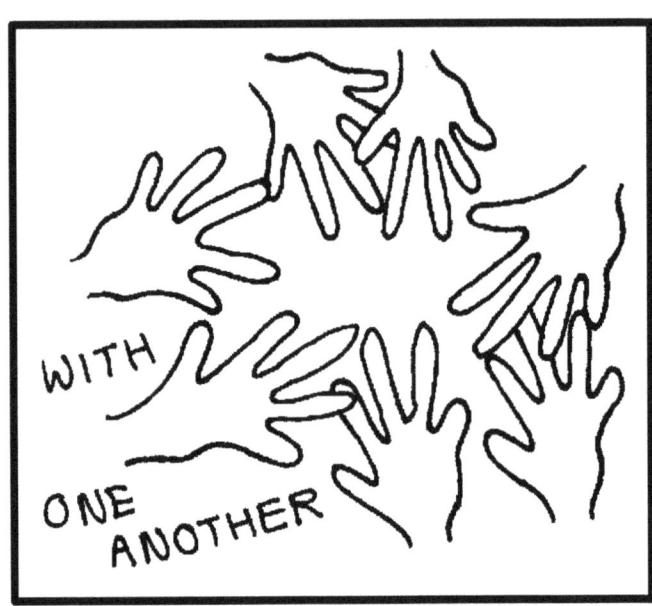

A FRIEND LIKE ME

RESPECT STORY

At a little farm house a little way from town lived a broom, a rake and a spade. The three had important jobs around the farm and thought that they were the most important tool that farmer Tom had. They would lie against the farm house wall looking out over beautiful fields and reflect on all the wonderful things that they could do. They never talked to each other though and sometimes they became quite lonely and sad. Each wished for a friend like themselves to talk to and pass the time when they were not needed by farmer Tom.

One day farmer Tom went on a holiday for a whole week.

For the first day they sat in silence thinking their usual thoughts of how they were so much better than the other two.

The second day they had happy thoughts about how one day they might have a friend just like themselves who did important work around the farm.

On the third day they all had sad thoughts about how nice it would be to have that friend right now.

On the fourth day they started to hum to themselves just to fill in the silence.

RESPECT
STORY

On the fifth day the spade started to cry big wet tears.
The broom turned to the spade looking very annoyed,
"Careful, you are wetting my bristles."
"What are you crying for anyway," queried the rake in a nasty tone.
"I want a friend just like me. Important, useful, and somewhere
close so that I can talk to it. It's soooo lonely." Moaned the spade.
There was silence for a bit and then the broom gave a sigh and
admitted slowly, "I was thinking exactly the same."
The rake eyed them both carefully and then said hesitantly, "Me too."
Then without saying a word they looked each other up.....
and then they looked each other down.
They tilted their heads on the side and looked
at each other that way and then tilted it to the
other side and looked at each other that way.

"So what can you do that is so important," said the broom to the rake.
"I rake up all the leaves so that the lawn is always beautiful and green
for the children to play on," the rake explained.
"Wow, that is pretty important, I can't do that," exclaimed the spade.
"What about you two," asked the rake, "what do you do that is so good.
"I sweep the verrandah so that the wind doesn't blow all the dirt into
the house." explained the broom.
"That's very clever, I could never do that. I dig the holes to put in new
vegetable plants which gives the farmer his food." said the spade proudly.
"That's amazing," exclaimed the broom and the rake at the same time.
"We are all important in different jobs." Said the spade,
his tears quite forgotten.
The spade the rake and the broom
chatted away until it got very dark.

Then when the sun came out on the sixth day they started chatting about all
their adventures. They talked so long that it got very, very dark.

On the seventh day as the sun came up who should come
down the road, but farmer Tom, back from his holiday,
The time had gone so quickly with all their talking
that they were all very surprised to see him.
From then on, at the end of each day they would
share the events of the day with each other and
listen admiringly to each others achievements.
Never again were they lonely. They each had two
great friends.

MORAL – Respecting people means overcoming differences and appreciating people for who they are.

OBEDIENCE

LESSON PLAN

DAY 1

PRAYER: Sing prayers that have been learnt and any others that the children know. Ask them to be reverent because they are talking to God.

STAR BOX: What is in the box? A plastic fish (relate it to the story)

STORY: "Yes Mummy"

DISCUSSION: What does obedience mean?
How does being obedient help our mum and dad?
If everyone did exactly what they wanted and didn't listen to the teach, what would happen to the classroom?
Optional - Use discussion points sheet at the beginning of the book to help discuss the meaning of obedience.

SONG: "Can You" - sing with actions.

QUOTE:

"O people be obedient to the ordinances of God"
   Bahá'u'lláh

Place the quotation in the letterbox as described in the beginning of the book. These are the messages God has sent us through special people. Ask a child to take out the letter.
Ask the children to say the quotation with you a couple of times. Discuss what it means.

Discussion - God gives us rules and guidance as to how we should live our lives and we did to be obedient and follow this guidance. We don't always fully understand the reason for why we need to do something but there is always a good reason and so we need to be obedient to it. It is the same as if a mother asks a young child to not run out on the road. When they are very little they don't know why their mother has said this but as the child get's older they come to understand the reason why.

ACTIVITY: Fish followers – Use activity sheet on the next page.
Purpose – to visualize virtue – to understand that obedience is following exactly what we are told even when we don't understand it.

DAY 2

PRAYER: Sing prayers that have been learnt and any others that the children know. Ask them to be reverent because they are talking to God.

SONG: "Can You" - sing with actions.

DISCUSSION REVIEW: What does obedience mean?

GAME: Everyone stands in a circle. One person starts by saying "Do as I Do" and then does an action. For example, patting the head. Everyone has to copy them. The person to the right of the one who started now repeats the same thing by saying "Do as I Do" and then an action. Keep moving around the circle. See how fast you can move from one person to the next.
Purpose – to practice being obedient by following the actions exactly.

QUOTE VISUALISATION:

"O people be obedient to the ordinances of God"
   Bahá'u'lláh

Photocopy the quote visualisation page. Go through the quote with the children to help them become familiar with the words and understand the meaning. Older children may be able to memorize it. Give each child a copy of the page to colour in. Choose an activity from the front of the book to present the quotations creatively.

OBEDIENCE
FISH FOLLOWERS

INSTRUCTIONS:
- Cut out the two fish and the quotation strip
- On to the big fish stick sequins or shiny paper to the fin and a small plastic eye to the head.
- Tape a fish on to either side of the quotation.
- Tape a pencil on to the back of the big fish.
- Colour in

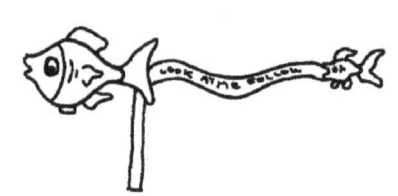

EACH CHILD WILL NEED:
- Glue, sticky tape
- Sequins or shiny paper
- Crayons / pencils and scissors
- A spare pencil or stick
- A photocopy of this page on to white A4 card.

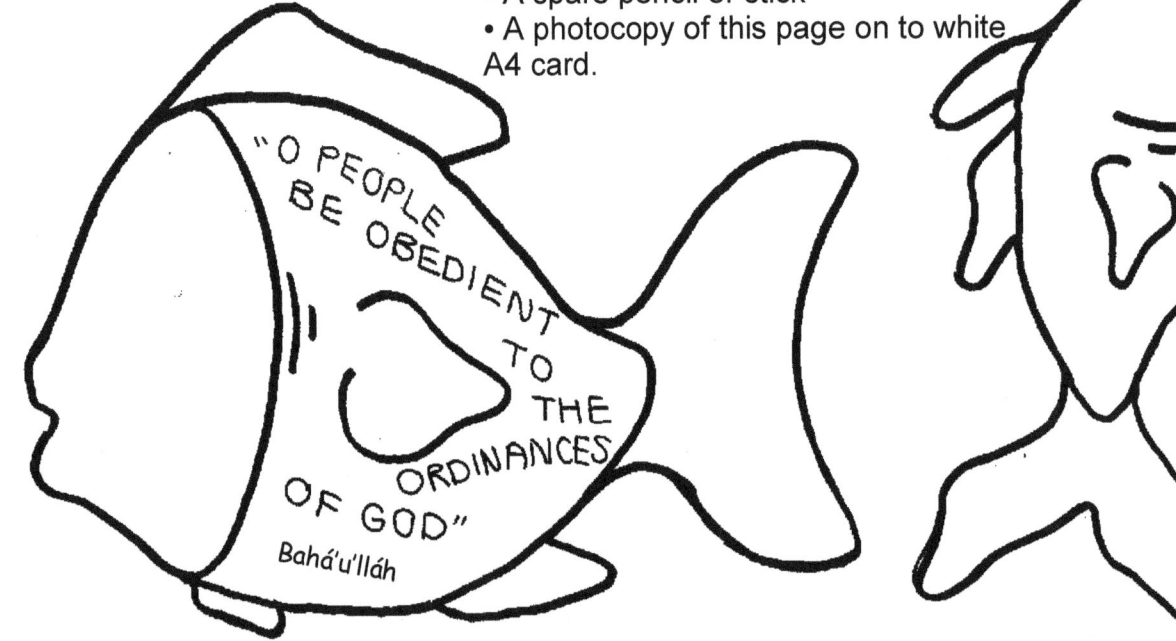

Quote Visualisation

OBEDIENCE

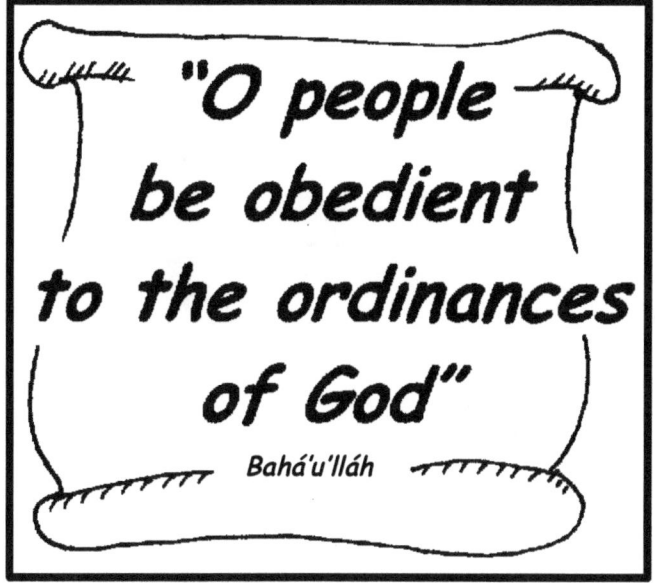

YES MUMMY

OBEDIENCE STORY

The water was lovely and calm in the ocean as six fish swam slowly through the water. The six fish lived among the rocks where they were protected from bigger fish who wanted to eat them, the strong water currents and the other dangers of the ocean. The fish swam in a line. First came the mummy, then the Báby, the little sister, the little brother, the big sister and finally the big brother.

Their mummy would warn them every morning before they went out. "You must always swim close to me and do exactly as I say. The ocean can be a dangerous place."
"Yes mummy," squeaked the Báby.
"Yes, Yes," spoke the little sister.
"As always," groaned the little brother.
"Of course mummy," screeched the big sister.
"You've told us before," huffed the big brother.

Then they would set out for a swim.
First they went past some slimy seaweed.
"Don't go too close to the seaweed, follow me," ordered mummy fish.
"Yes mummy," squeaked the Báby.
"Yes, Yes," spoke the little sister.
"As always," groaned the little brother.
"Of course mummy," screeched the big sister.
But big brother didn't say anything because he had swum very close to the seaweed and a great big octopus had swiped him up with his long arms and gobbled him up.

OBEDIENCE STORY

Then they swam past a net.
"Don't go too close to the net, follow me," ordered mummy fish.
"Yes mummy," squeaked the Báby.
"Yes, Yes," spoke the little sister.
"As always," groaned the little brother.
But no-one else said anything because big sister had swum right over the net just as a fisherman had pulled the string tight and hauled the net out of the water with big sister in it.

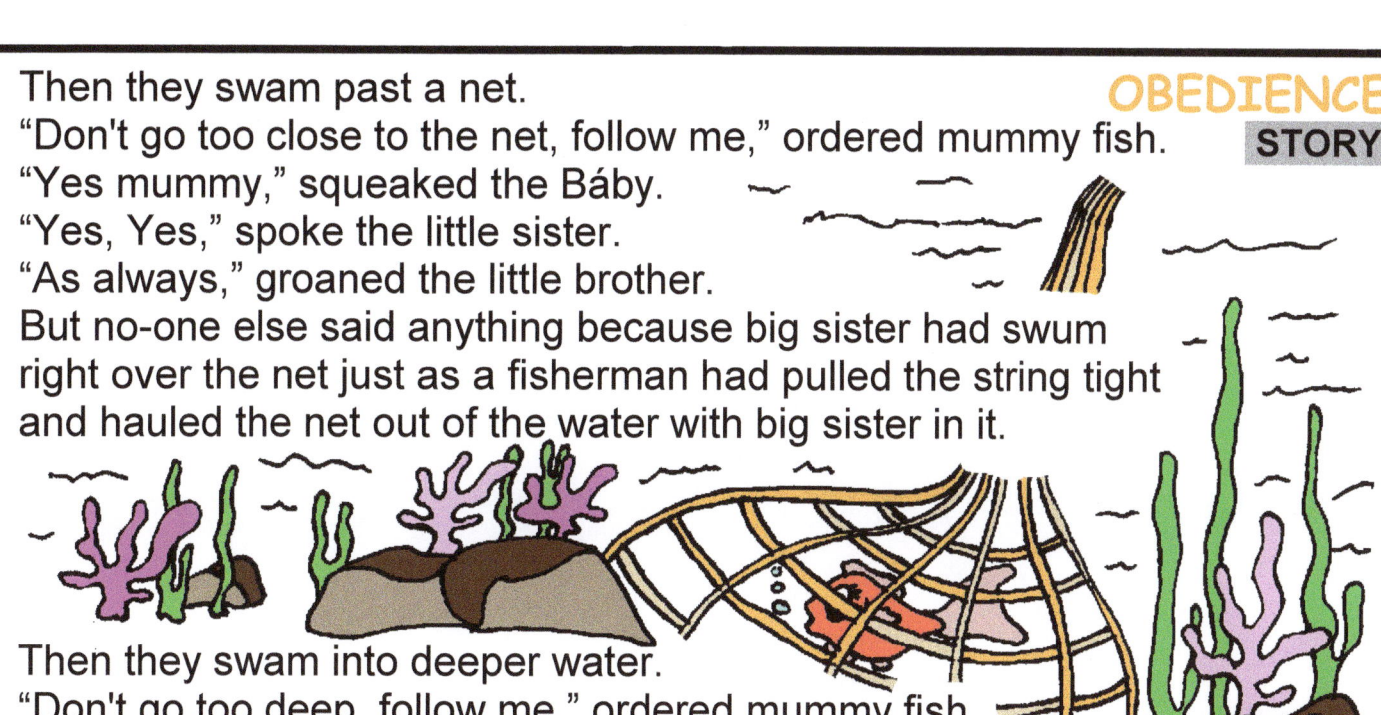

Then they swam into deeper water.
"Don't go too deep, follow me," ordered mummy fish.
"Yes mummy," squeaked the Báby.
"Yes, Yes," spoke the little sister.
But no-one else said anything because little brother had swum straight toward the biggest part of the ocean where the water moved very fast and he was washed away in a great big wave.

Then they swam up close to the surface.
"Don't jump out of the water, follow me," ordered mummy fish.
"Yes mummy," squeaked the Báby.
But no-one else said anything because little sister had jumped right out of the water and a bird picked her up in his big beak and swallowed her down whole.

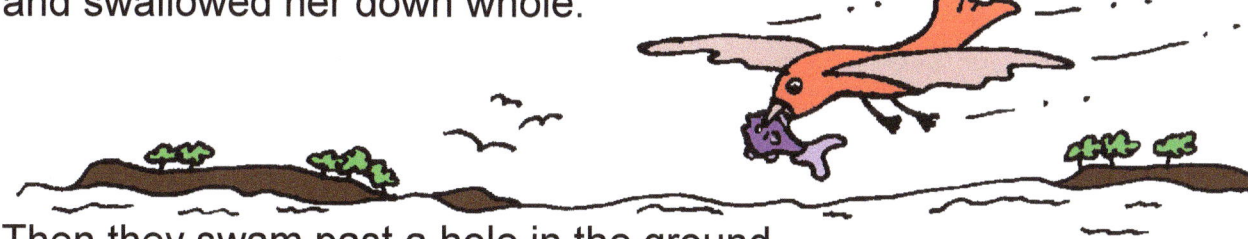

Then they swam past a hole in the ground.
"Don't go near the hole, follow me," ordered mummy fish.
"Yes mummy," squeaked the Báby just as a huge crab put out its claw ready to grab something. But it didn't get anything because the Báby fish had listened to its mother and stayed right behind her just as she had asked.

MORAL – Obedience is following instructions even when we don't understand.

LOVE

LESSON PLAN

DAY 1

PRAYER: Sing prayers that have been learnt and any others that the children know. Ask them to be reverent because they are talking to God.

STAR BOX: What is in the box? Money (relate it to the story)

STORY: "Treasure Hunt"

DISCUSSION: What does love mean?
 What could we say to show love to other people?
 What could we do to show love to other people?
 Optional - Use discussion points sheet at the beginning of the book to help discuss the meaning of love.

SONG: "Love Is A Treasure" - sing with actions.

QUOTE:
 "Make My love thy treasure and cherish it even as thy very sight and life"
  Bahá'u'lláh
 Place the quotation in the letterbox as described in the beginning of the book. These are the messages God has sent us through special people. Ask a child to take out the letter.
 Ask the children to say the quotation with you a couple of times. Discuss what it means.

 Discussion - Some people hold on to money, fancy cars or expensive toys and think that they are more important than anything else, but love is our greatest treasure. Toys cars and money break, get used up, get lost or turn back into the dust they came from but love lasts forever and gives us happiness when all these other things are gone.

ACTIVITY: Treasure chests – Use activity sheet on the next page.
 Purpose – to visualize quotation – to understand that love is the greatest treasure of all.

DAY 2

PRAYER: Sing prayers that have been learnt and any others that the children know. Ask them to be reverent because they are talking to God.

SONG: "Love Is A Treasure" - sing with actions.

DISCUSSION REVIEW: What does love mean?

GAME: Prepare a treasure chest from the activity in Day 1. Divide the class into pairs. Each person has a turn of writing one thing they love about their partner and then put it into the treasure chest with a small sweet or lolly. Then they go and hide it somewhere and ask their partner to find it. Ask the children to write one thing they love about someone else in the class.
 Purpose – To think about the things we can love people for.

QUOTE VISUALISATION:
 "Make My love thy treasure and cherish it even as thy very sight and life"
  Bahá'u'lláh
 Photocopy the quote visualisation page. Go through the quote with the children to help them become familiar with the words and understand the meaning. Older children may be able to memorize it. Give each child a copy of the page to colour in. Choose an activity from the front of the book to present the quotations creatively.

INSTRUCTIONS:
- Cut out the treasure chest
- Colour in
- Fold along dotted lines
- Glue in marked places (tape if needed)
- Curl the lid slightly to make a curved shape.
- Cut, colour and glue the quotation into the inside of the box.

EACH CHILD WILL NEED:
- Scissors, glue, sticky tape
- Crayons / pencils
- A photocopy of this page on to white card.

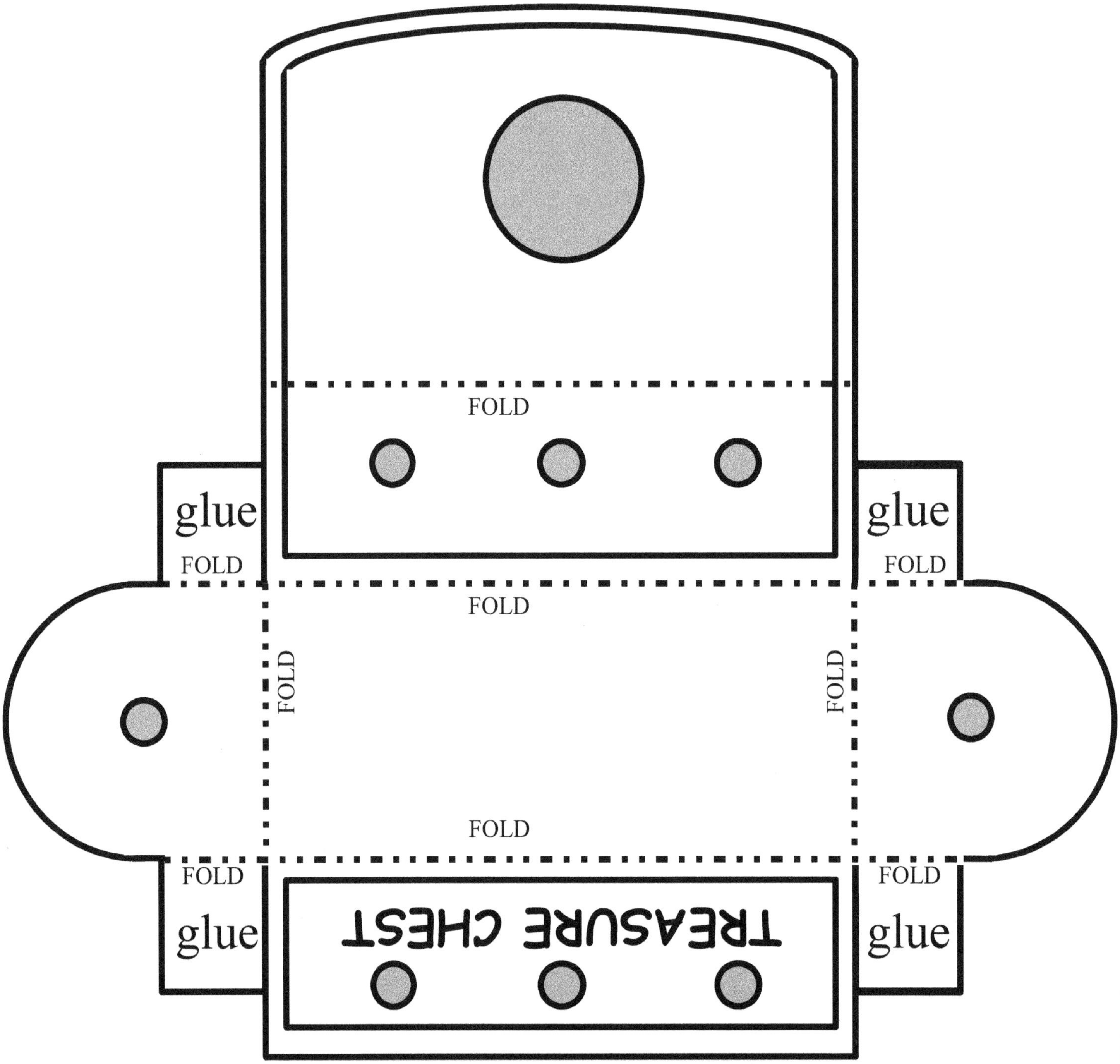

LOVE
TREASURE CHESTS

"Make My love thy treasure and cherish it even as thy very sight and life." *Bahá'u'lláh*

Quote Visualisation LOVE

TREASURE HUNT

There were once three children who were always fighting with each other.
They yelled and hit and said nasty things to each other.
One day they found a treasure map.
"OOOh," exclaimed Sally.
"Aaah," said Patrick.
"Eeeeh," squeaked Sam.

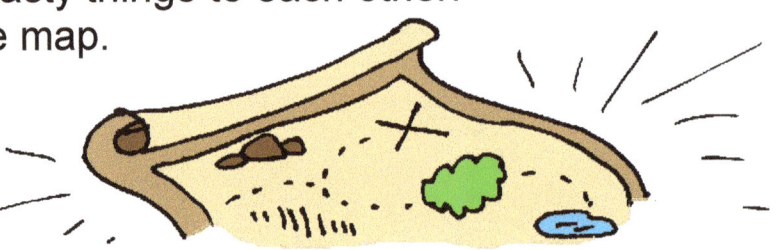

They followed the directions on the map to a big forest. It was very dark.
"We all better hold hands or we will lose each other" said Sam.
"I'm not holding hands with you," whined Patrick and Sally and then they all split up, walking in different directions.
It felt even darker on their own.
"Patrick," yelled Sally.
"Sam," screamed Patrick.
"Sally," whimpered Sam.
They were all very scared and wished they weren't alone.

Sally came to a dark tunnel and slowly crept through with her knees shaking. She thought she could smell something nasty.

Sam came to a creek and waded through deep water with his teeth chattering loudly. He thought he felt something swimming around his legs.

Patrick came to some tall rustling reeds and tip-toed through quietly with his hands shivering. He thought he heard some animal noises.

They all screamed loudly.
Sally ran back through the tunnel and out of the forest.
Sam crawled out of the creek and back out of the forest.
Patrick pushed himself back through the reeds and raced out of the forest.

They all bumped into each other and clung together tightly.
"I lost the map," gasped Sam.
"Who cares about any treasure anyway," said Sally when she had caught her breath.
"Seeing you two was better than any jewels or diamonds," sighed Patrick.
They all smiled at each other and agreed. Having each other was the best treasure of all.

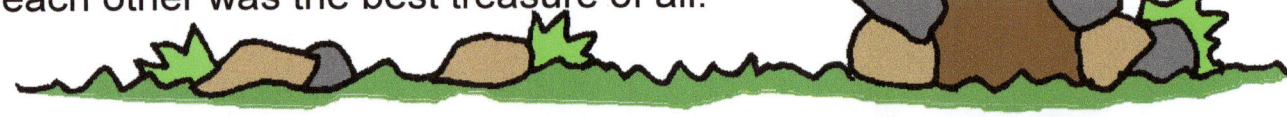

MORAL – Love is the greatest treasure that we can have.

PRAYERFULNESS

LESSON PLAN

DAY 1

PRAYER: Sing prayers that have been learnt and any others that the children know. Ask them to be reverent because they are talking to God.

STAR BOX: What is in the box? A cotton wool bud (relate it to the story)

STORY: "Cloe's Clouds"

DISCUSSION: What does prayerfulness mean?
Just because we are saying prayers doesn't mean we are being prayerful. Being prayerful is about how we feel inside.
Can we only be prayerful when we are saying a prayer?
Optional - Use discussion points sheet at the beginning of the book to help discuss the meaning of prayerfulness.

SONG: "God Will Be There Too" - sing with actions.

QUOTE:
"... strive that your actions day by day may be beautiful prayers."
'Abdu'l-Bahá
Place the quotation in the letterbox as described in the beginning of the book. These are the messages God has sent us through special people. Ask a child to take out the letter.
Ask the children to say the quotation with you a couple of times. Discuss what it means.

Discussion - Being prayerful is not just about saying the words of a prayer. Being prayerful means to make the things that we do like prayers. When we say prayers we ask God for guidance and he guides us. When we act out these prayers in our lives and think of God then God will always be with us. Prayerfulness is about what we are feeling and thinking inside ourselves when we are doing things.

ACTIVITY: Ayyam-i-Ha Calendars – Use activity sheet on the next page.
Purpose – to reflect on quotation – to understand that prayerfulness is not just sitting down saying words. It is an attitude that can help us in every day things. It is something from within.
NOTE: THIS ACTIVITY IS ONLY FOR CHILDREN WHOSE FAMILIES CELEBRATE AYYAM-I-HA AND IT SHOULD BE DONE ONE WEEK BEFORE AYYAM-I-HA.

DAY 2

PRAYER: Sing prayers that have been learnt and any others that the children know. Ask them to be reverent because they are talking to God.

SONG: "God Will Be There Too" - sing with actions.

DISCUSSION REVIEW: What does prayerfulness mean?

GAME: Tell everyone to shut their eyes and forget about all the things that happened that day or the day before or are going to happen later. Ask them to focus only on the sounds they can hear. After a couple of minutes ask everyone to open their eyes and talk about what they could hear. Purpose - to use a prayerful attitude while listening only to the sounds.

QUOTE VISUALISATION:
"... strive that your actions day by day may be beautiful prayers."
'Abdu'l-Bahá
Photocopy the quote visualisation page. Go through the quote with the children to help them become familiar with the words and understand the meaning. Older children may be able to memorize it. Give each child a copy of the page to colour in. Choose an activity from the front of the book to present the quotations creatively.

INSTRUCTIONS:
- Photocopy this page on to different coloured papers
- Use a craft knife to cut along the top, bottom and right hand side of each door with a star.
- Cut along the dotted lines and give each child a copy of the part with the numbers and the part with the quote (two different colours).
- Cut along the thick dark line which borders the part with the quote.
- Glue the quote part on top of the number part without gluing down the doors (do not open the doors).
- Colour in doors
- Glue a magnet on to the back so that it can sit on the fridge.
- For the week preceding Ayyam-i-há one door is opened up each day

EACH CHILD WILL NEED:
- Scissors, glue for paper and strong glue for
- Crayons / pencils
- Craft knife (adult use only)
- Coloured card
- A magnet

PRAYERFULNESS
AYYAM-I–HÁ CALENDARS

"... strive that your actions day by day may be beautiful prayers."
'Abdu'l-Bahá

COUNT DOWN TO AYYAM-I-HÁ

Quote Visualisation

PRAYERFULNESS

CLOE'S CLOUDS

PRAYERFULNESS STORY

Cloe sat down to breakfast and gazed out the window. It was a beautiful day and she couldn't wait to get outside.

Mum announced, "Let's say a prayer before you go out."

"Oh, I'm no good at prayers," complained Cloe, "It's too hard and I always get distracted."

All through the prayer Cloe kept looking out the window.

As soon as the prayer was finished she ran outside and lay down on a favorite spot under a tree. She looked straight up and watched some birds flying in and out of their nest. Then she remained very still and watched a lizard crawl over her hand. She hid behind a bush while a spider spun its web and then followed a line of ants as they took food to their nest.

Finally, exhausted she lay on the ground and gazed up at the sky. It was very blue and the hot sun made her feel sleepy. Mum came out and sat beside her but she barely noticed.

"The clouds all look like bunny rabbits today," said Cloe wistfully.

"Yes," whispered mum, "and you are being very prayerful."

"How," asked Cloe surprised, "I'm just looking at clouds."

Being prayerful is many things. It is sometimes enjoying being quiet and still. Tomorrow we will say our prayers outside."

"Can we do that," queried Cloe.

"Of course," said Mum.

The next day Cloe sat with her back against a tree, closed her eyes and felt the wind rustle her hair. She listened to the words as mum read from a prayer book. Cloe smiled, it was good being prayerful. She settled down to watch the clouds.

"I think they are smiling at me today" said Cloe happily.

"I think so too" said Mum as they both gazed up at the sky in silence.

MORAL – Prayerfulness is not just about saying words it is also about how you feel inside.

UNITY

LESSON PLAN

DAY 1

PRAYER: Sing prayers that have been learnt and any others that the children know. Ask them to be reverent because they are talking to God.

STAR BOX: What is in the box? Some salad – Relate it to the story

STORY: "A Colourful Salad"

DISCUSSION: What does unity mean?
How can we use unity to help us build a house?
Would would happen to the house if people are not in unity?
Optional - Use discussion points sheet at the beginning of the book to help discuss the meaning of unity.

SONG: "Unity" - sing with actions

QUOTE:

"So powerful is the light of unity that it can illuminate the whole earth."
    Bahá'u'lláh

Place the quotation in the letterbox as described in the beginning of the book. These are the messages God has sent us through special people. Ask a child to take out the letter.
Ask the children to say the quotation with you a couple of times. Discuss what it means.

Discussion - When we work alone we can only do little things but when we work together we can accomplish things we never thought possible. The power unity has is far stronger than anything else and has the ability to bring all the different peoples of the world together in harmony. There have been many wars, fighting and conflict between countries and peoples, wouldn't it be wonderful if all this stopped and people lived together happily.

ACTIVITY: Strong Men – Use activity sheet on the next page.
Purpose – to reflect on quotation – to understand the power unity has and how much stronger people are when they stand together. We can do in unity with others what we cannot do by ourselves.

DAY 2

PRAYER: Sing prayers that have been learnt and any others that the children know. Ask them to be reverent because they are talking to God.

SONG: "Unity" - sing with actions

DISCUSSION REVIEW: What does unity mean?

GAME: Everyone hold hands in a circle and at the same time hop on one leg. To make it harder, try hopping around in a circle while still holding hands.
Purpose – to work together in unity. If there is no unity everyone will fall down.

QUOTE VISUALISATION:

"So powerful is the light of unity that it can illuminate the whole earth."
    Bahá'u'lláh

Photocopy the quote visualisation page. Go through the quote with the children to help them become familiar with the words and understand the meaning. Older children may be able to memorize it. Give each child a copy of the page to colour in. Choose an activity from the front of the book to present the quotations creatively.

UNITY
STRONG MEN

STEP 1.
Fold a white A4 page in half lengthwise

STEP 2.
Fold both sides backwards on itself

STEP 3.
Cut into thirds. One third per child.

STEP 4.
Cut out template and draw around it, then cut along outline. Unfold.

EACH CHILD WILL NEED:
- A copy of a template on card.
- Scissors
- Crayons / pencils
- A piece of white paper.

STEP 5.
Colour in men.
Keep the men folded into one and it cannot stand up.
Unfold them and they can stand up.
Alone we are weak, together in unity we are strong.

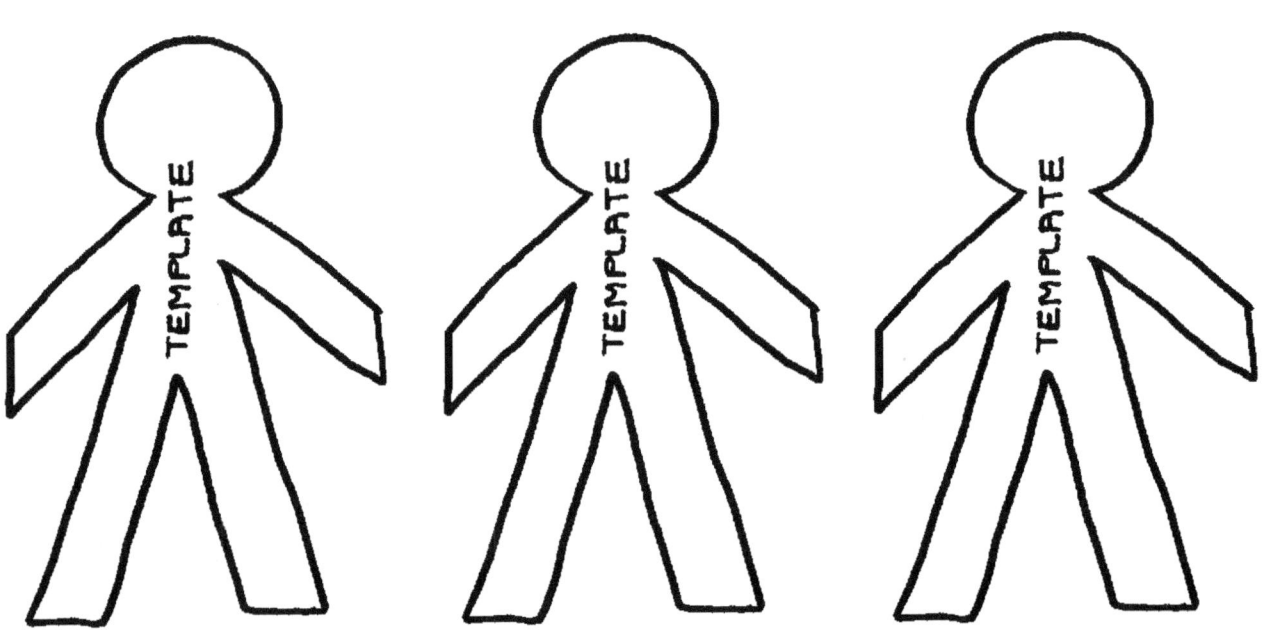

UNITY

Quote Visualisation

"So powerful is the light of unity that it can illuminate the whole earth."
— Bahá'u'lláh

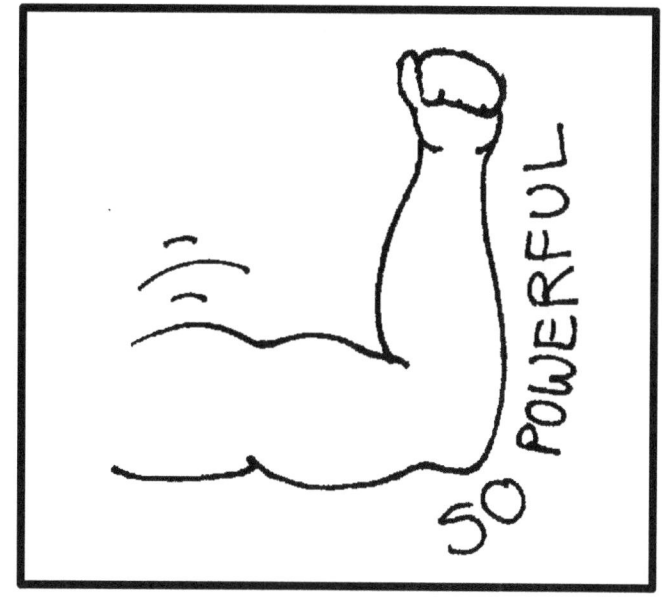

A COLOURFUL SALAD

It was a rainy, wet evening and the vegetables in the garden were soaking up the water. The family of the house next to the garden were eating their dinner on the verandah. Lettuce was looking gloomily at the three people eating.
"She never eats her greens," complained Lettuce.
"Who's not eating salad," asked Carrot with interest.
"Little Lisa who lives in the house," replied Lettuce.
"No use thinking about that," stated Tomato grumpily.
"It's got nothing to do with us."
"No, we can't do anything about that," agreed Cucumber gruffly.
The vegetables all went back to soaking up the water for a while without saying anything.

"Yes we can," said the Carrot excitedly.
The other vegetables looked at him doubtfully.
"Little Lisa is only ever given one vegetable at a time," explained Carrot. "What if her salad had the crisp greenness of Lettuce, the juicy redness of Tomato, the fresh crunchiness of Cucumber and the orange sweetness of me."
"That might work," said Lettuce thoughtfully.
During the next two days the vegetables focused all their energy on soaking up water and sunshine so that they were the very best they could be.

When the lady of the house came to get some food for dinner she picked a little from each plant.
That night the vegetables watched intently as the family sat down to dinner. Lisa was served up a big colourful bowel of salad.
The vegetables watched as she looked at the salad. Then she nibbled on a piece of carrot, took a bite from a slice of cucumber, tasted a leaf of lettuce and sucked on some tomato. Then she smiled, picked up her fork and ate the whole bowl so quickly that the vegetables couldn't believe their eyes.
"We make a great team," said Tomato proudly and they all nodded in agreement.

MORAL - Unity means together you can do things that on your own you cannot.

JUSTICE

LESSON PLAN

DAY 1

PRAYER: Sing prayers that have been learnt and any others that the children know. Ask them to be reverent because they are talking to God.

STAR BOX: What is in the box? A cardboard crown (relate it to the story)

STORY: "The Greatest Crown"

DISCUSSION: What does justice mean?
If there is one piece of cake and two people then how could we use justice to make both people happy?
How would these two people feel when the cake has been divided fairly between them?
Optional - Use discussion points sheet at the beginning of the book to help discuss the meaning of justice.

SONG: "Crown Of Jewels" - sing with actions.

QUOTE:
"Attire mine head with the crown of justice...."
    Bahá'u'lláh
Place the quotation in the letterbox as described in the beginning of the book. These are the messages God has sent us through special people. Ask a child to take out the letter.
Ask the children to say the quotation with you a couple of times. Discuss what it means.

Discussion - Lot's of people want to where a crown and be a king or queen but often these people treat the people under them unfairly. They allow some to get away with wrong things and make them rich and wealthy while others who are good hearted are pushed aside and left without a proper home or food. They so much want to where their crown but they forget to also put on the crown of justice. Justice is what makes things fair for everyone.

ACTIVITY: Crown of Justice – Use activity sheet on the next page.
Purpose – to reflect on quotation – to understand that justice makes us better people. Being fair makes us noble people.

DAY 2

PRAYER: Sing prayers that have been learnt and any others that the children know. Ask them to be reverent because they are talking to God.

SONG: "Crown Of Jewels" - sing with actions.

DISCUSSION REVIEW: What does justice mean?

GAME: Read out a set of instructions. Each person has to follow the instructions to create a picture, eg. Draw a circle as big as the page, draw a smaller circle into the middle of the bigger circle.
Purpose – to show how we have rules for a purpose. Even if we don't understand each rule. They are there to keep things just for everyone.

QUOTE VISUALISATION:
"Attire mine head with the crown of justice...."
    Bahá'u'lláh
Photocopy the quote visualisation page. Go through the quote with the children to help them become familiar with the words and understand the meaning. Older children may be able to memorize it. Give each child a copy of the page to colour in. Choose an activity from the front of the book to present the quotations creatively.

JUSTICE
CROWN OF JUSTICE

"ATTIRE MINE HEAD WITH THE CROWN OF JUSTICE..."
Bahá'u'lláh

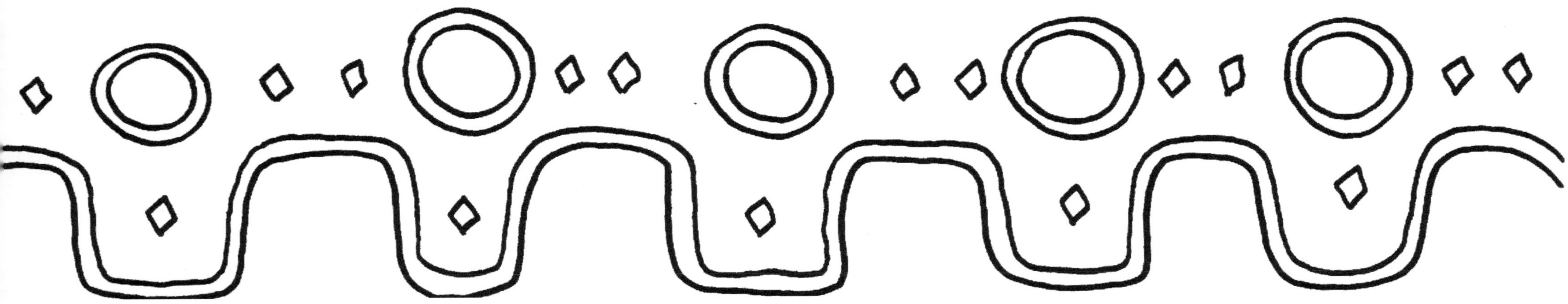

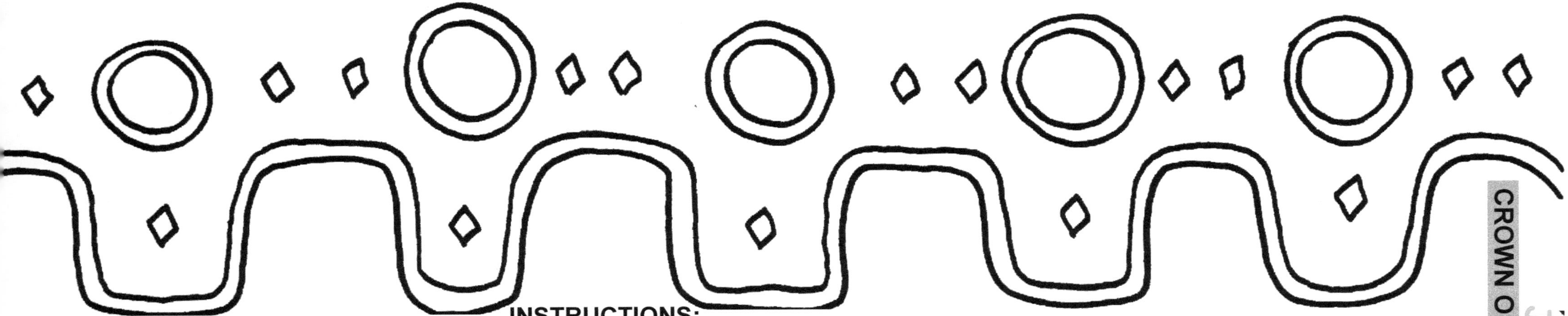

INSTRUCTIONS:
- Photocopy this sheet on to card.
- Cut out the two crown pieces
- Tape them together on the back
- Glue shiny pieces of paper on to the crown
- Colour in
- Fit crown to head size and tape together.

EACH CHILD WILL NEED:
- Scissors, glue, sticky tape
- One piece of white card.
- Shiny pieces of paper
- Crayons / pencils

Quote Visualisation　　　　　　　　　　　　　　　　　　　　　　　　JUSTICE

THE GREATEST CROWN

JUSTICE STORY

There was once a wise man named Lorenzo. He stood next to a little boy who gazed at the King who sat in his carriage as it drove down the street. The King stopped nearby to survey his city. Close to the king was a shopkeeper called Simon. Lorenzo the wise man pointed out the king and the shopkeeper, asking the boy, "Who wears the greatest crown?" The boy frowned at him, "The King of course, the shopkeeper wears nothing on his head but that old hat." "Watch," said Lorenzo.

A little while later the King spied a bag of sweets sitting near the shop window. Seeing that no-one was watching he grabbed the sweets like a practiced thief and hid them in his pocket. Just then a lady came by to buy some food at the shop.

Simon the shopkeeper noticed the missing sweets.
"I have been robbed," cried Simon.
The King with a smirk on his face pointed to the lady and said loudly, "There's the thief, take her away guards."
Before the guards could move Simon shouted,
"NO, she is not the one who took my sweets."
The frightened lady looked first at one and then the other.
"Do you dare speak against the King," boomed the King.
"No, not the king, only the thief." replied Simon sternly.
"You could be a good King, but right now you are a bad thief."
The King was silent for a moment and then nodded his head slowly.
"You are right, I am a bad thief, now I will go and become a good King."
He placed the sweets in Simon's hand and walked back to his carriage preparing for the drive back to his castle.

Lorenzo the wise man looked down at the little boy and asked again, "Who wears the greatest crown?"
The boy smiled and replied confidently, "Simon the shopkeeper wears the crown of justice which shines even more brightly than the jewels in the Kings golden crown."
The boy looked back to where Lorenzo had been standing but he was gone. The boy had answered right.

MORAL – Justice makes us more noble than any king.

CONFIDENCE

LESSON PLAN

DAY 1

PRAYER: Sing prayers that have been learnt and any others that the children know. Ask them to be reverent because they are talking to God.

STAR BOX: What is in the box? A sheet of music (relate it to the story)

STORY: "I Can"

DISCUSSION: What does confidence mean?
Confidence helps us to have a go at things when something feels scary or difficult.
Optional - Use discussion points sheet at the beginning of the book to help discuss the meaning of confidence.

SONG: "I Feel Confident" - sing with actions.

QUOTE:
"...place your whole trust and confidence in God."
    Bahá'u'lláh

Place the quotation in the letterbox as described in the beginning of the book. These are the messages God has sent us through special people. Ask a child to take out the letter.
Ask the children to say the quotation with you a couple of times. Discuss what it means.

Discussion - When we are feeling scared or worried about something we can ask God to help us and he will give us the strength to deal with any difficult thing we have to do.

ACTIVITY: Confidence bags – Use activity sheet on the next page.
Purpose – to reflect on virtue – to understand some of the ways in which we can be confident. To understand that God can help us be confidant when we are afraid. We just have to trust in Him.

DAY 2

PRAYER: Sing prayers that have been learnt and any others that the children know. Ask them to be reverent because they are talking to God.

SONG: "I Feel Confident" - sing with actions.

DISCUSSION REVIEW: What does confidence mean?

GAME: Each person stands up and spends 30 seconds giving a little speech about their favorite game.
Purpose – to practice using confidence.

QUOTE VISUALISATION:
"...place your whole trust and confidence in God."
    Bahá'u'lláh

Photocopy the quote visualisation page. Go through the quote with the children to help them become familiar with the words and understand the meaning. Older children may be able to memorize it. Give each child a copy of the page to colour in. Choose an activity from the front of the book to present the quotations creatively.

CONFIDENCE
CONFIDENCE BAGS

HANDLE

STEP 1.
Fold the edges of a piece of paper lengthwise in about 2 cm on each side.

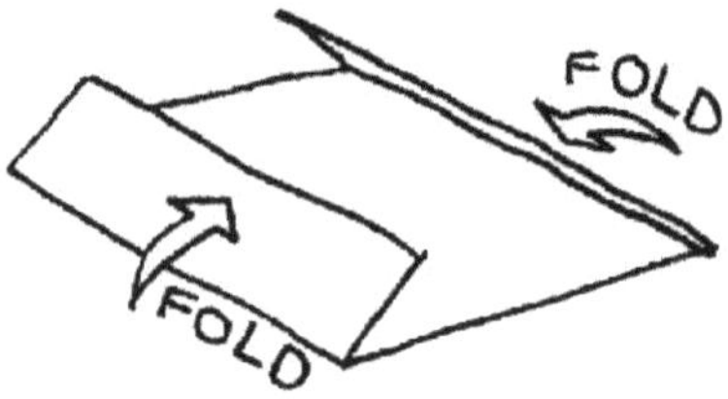

STEP 2.
Fold it in half

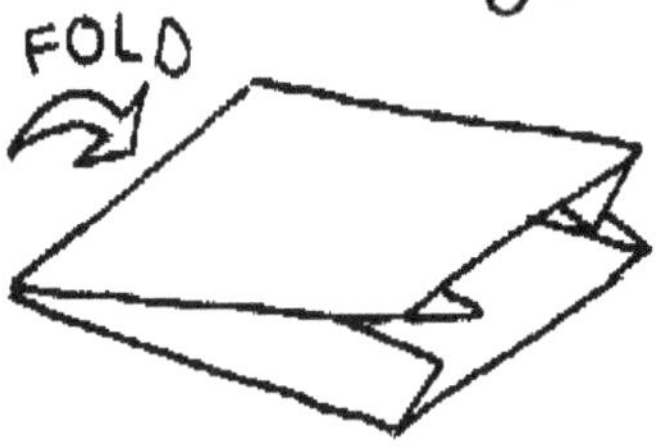

STEP 3.
Cut along the dotted lines of this page.

STEP 4.
Staple the two folded edges and the handle together. Glue the quotation to the front of the bag.

STEP 5.
Fill in the three things that you think you can be confident in.
Place them in the bag.

EACH CHILD WILL NEED:
- Scissors, glue, crayons
- Stapler (adult use only)
- This page copied on white card.
- A piece of coloured paper.

CUT
CUT
CUT

"...place your trust and confidence in God"
— Bahá'u'lláh

I AM CONFIDENT AT:

I AM CONFIDENT AT:

I AM CONFIDENT AT:

CONFIDENCE

Quote Visualisation

KINDNESS

LESSON PLAN

DAY 1

PRAYER: Sing prayers that have been learnt and any others that the children know. Ask them to be reverent because they are talking to God.

STAR BOX: What is in the box? A map (relate it to the story)

STORY: "David's Journey"

DISCUSSION: What does kindness mean?
Who can we show kindness to?
How can we show kindness to someone who is younger and smaller than us?
Optional - Use discussion points sheet at the beginning of the book to help discuss the meaning of kindness.

SONG: "Kindness Time" - sing with actions.

QUOTE:
"... let your heart burn with loving kindness for all who may cross your path."
    'Abdu'l-Bahá

Place the quotation in the letterbox as described in the beginning of the book. These are the messages God has sent us through special people. Ask a child to take out the letter.
Ask the children to say the quotation with you a couple of times. Discuss what it means.

Discussion - Kindness is not something that we only give to some people. Kindness is a thing we can share with everyone we meet. It comes from our heart and can be shared through helping someone out, thinking of someone or even just smiling at anyone who passes you.

ACTIVITY: Lanterns – Use activity sheet on the next page.
Purpose – to visualize virtue – to understand how kindness can effect people around us. We should be kind to everyone, no matter who they are.

DAY 2

PRAYER: Sing prayers that have been learnt and any others that the children know. Ask them to be reverent because they are talking to God.

SONG: "Crown of Jewels" - sing with actions.

DISCUSSION REVIEW: What does kindness mean?

GAME: Everyone walks in different directions around the room. Every time someone gently bumps into someone else you have to shake their hand and say something like "It is very nice to meet you". Purpose – To visualize what it means to be kind to everyone who crosses your path.

QUOTE VISUALISATION:
"... let your heart burn with loving kindness for all who may cross your path."
    'Abdu'l-Bahá

Photocopy the quote visualisation page. Go through the quote with the children to help them become familiar with the words and understand the meaning. Older children may be able to memorize it. Give each child a copy of the page to colour in. Choose an activity from the front of the book to present the quotations creatively.

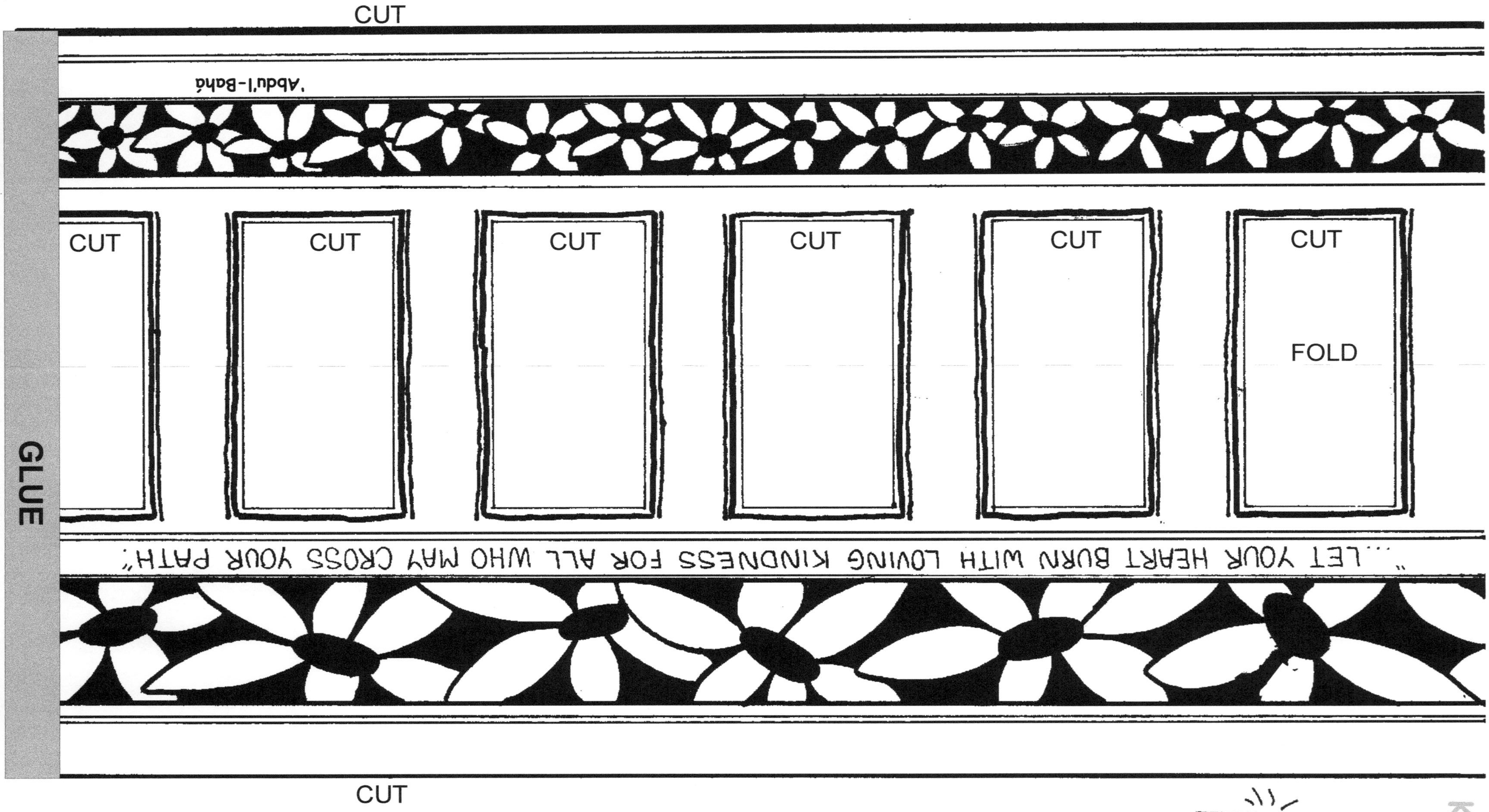

KINDNESS LANTERNS

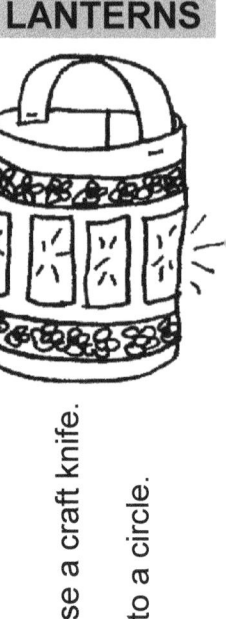

"...LET YOUR HEART BURN WITH LOVING KINDNESS FOR ALL WHO MAY CROSS YOUR PATH."

'Abdu'l-Bahá

EACH CHILD WILL NEED:
- Scissors, glue
- White card
- Crayons / pencils
- Stapler (for adult use only)
- Cellophane

INSTRUCTIONS:
- Photocopy this sheet on to white card and cut out the lantern.
- Fold along the marked line and cut out the windows where marked or use a craft knife.
- Unfold and colour in.
- Glue cellophane onto the inside of the windows then glue the lantern into a circle.
- Cut a strip of card for a handle and staple on.

Quote Visualisation KINDNESS

DAVID'S JOURNEY

KINDNESS STORY

David was an adventurous boy who decided to go on a journey.
First he headed North and came across a town where the people were as tall as his nose. His feet were big in comparison and he had to be careful not to step on them.
"Help, help," screamed a little lady suddenly, "A dragon is attacking me."
David knelt down gently, took a deep breath and blew as hard as he could at the dragon. The dragon got blown far away and he never returned.
"Thankyou so much," the lady called after him as he continued on his journey, this time heading East.

He soon came across a new town where thundering giants lived. This time he was the one who had to dodge between huge feet.
"Oh, Oh, I can't get it, Oh Ohhh..." cried a giant as if being tortured.
"What's wrong." I yelled up to him as loud as I could.
"I have an itch in the middle of my back that I just can't reach," whined the giant.
I climbed up his leg and over his back until I reached the spot that he pointed at. I then rubbed as hard as I could.
"I'll never forget you," he called after me as I continued on my journey, this time heading South.

After walking for some time I came across a town full of hairy monsters. They had big teeth but I bravely looked around anyway.
"Wahhh, Wahhhh" cried a Báby monster.
I wandered up and asked the lady holding it what the matter was.
"I don't know," she replied in a desperate voice, "It won't stop crying."
I looked down at the Báby then gently tickled its toes.
The Báby fell silent. I tickled its belly. The Báby smiled. I tickled its chin.
The Báby started laughing. As I walked off westward toward home, the laughter of the Báby continued on and on and on.

MORAL – Kindness can be shown to anyone no matter who they are.

COURTESY

LESSON PLAN

DAY 1

PRAYER: Sing prayers that have been learnt and any others that the children know. Ask them to be reverent because they are talking to God.

STAR BOX: What is in the box? A medallion / important badge or a toy mouse (relate it to the story)

STORY: "Lord of the Animals"

DISCUSSION: What does courtesy mean?
What words do we use when we are being courteous?
Courtesy is not just saying please and thankyou. It also means to say the words in a nice way.
Optional - Use discussion points sheet at the beginning of the book to help discuss the meaning of courtesy

SONG: "Courtesy" - sing with actions.

QUOTE:
"O people of God!... Courtesy is... the lord of all virtues"
　　Bahá'u'lláh
Place the quotation in the letterbox as described in the beginning of the book. These are the messages God has sent us through special people. Ask a child to take out the letter.
Ask the children to say the quotation with you a couple of times. Discuss what it means.

Discussion - Amongst all the virtues that we need to develop in ourselves courtesy is the lord or them all. It gives everything else we do, think and say meaning. Courtesy is a way of respecting others, being thoughtful of others and of showing others that we care.

ACTIVITY: Badge of Courtesy – Use activity sheet on the next page.
Purpose – to reflect on the virtue – to understand that courtesy makes us noble beings.

DAY 2

PRAYER: Sing prayers that have been learnt and any others that the children know. Ask them to be reverent because they are talking to God.

SONG: "In My Heart" - sing with actions.

DISCUSSION REVIEW: What does courtesy mean?

GAME: Play a game of courtesy bingo. Read out a question from those provided or make up your own. The first person to call out the right answer can put a cross in one of their boxes. Whoever fills in all their boxes first and calls out bingo, wins the game. Use the game provided.
Purpose – to increase familiarity with what courteous means.

QUOTE VISUALISATION:
"O people of God!... Courtesy is... the lord of all virtues"
　　Bahá'u'lláh
Photocopy the quote visualisation page. Go through the quote with the children to help them become familiar with the words and understand the meaning. Older children may be able to memorize it. Give each child a copy of the page to colour in. Choose an activity from the front of the book to present the quotations creatively.

INSTRUCTIONS:
- Photocopy this page on to white card
- Cut out badge
- Colour in
- Decorate with glitter pens or metallic pens
- Stick ribbons on to back with tape.
- Tape a safety pin on to back.

EACH CHILD WILL NEED:
- Scissors, sticky tape
- Glitter pens / metallic pens
- Crayons / pencils
- White card
- Two wide pieces of ribbon and one thin one about 4 cm long each.
- One small safety pin

COURTESY
BADGE OF COURTESY

Quote Visualisation

COURTESY

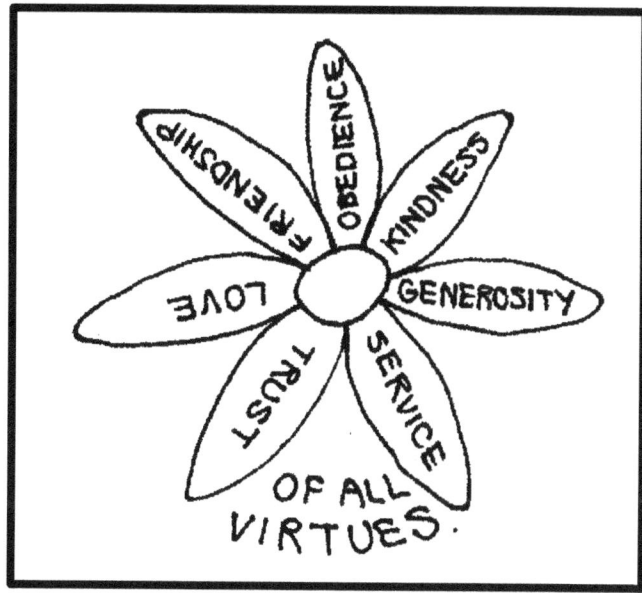

COURTESY

Game
Bingo boards – cut out one for each child.

88

COURTESY

Game

BINGO QUESTIONS

- What would you say if someone gave you a birthday present?
- What should you say when you ask someone for a drink?
- What do you say when you want to get through a door but someone is standing in the way?
- What do you say if you accidentally step on someone's foot?
- What would you say when someone says hello?
- What could you say when you are leaving after playing at someone's house?
- What should you use to eat your dinner?
- How do we sit on a chair at the table?
- How should we sit when we are saying prayers?
- What should we do if there are only three cups but four people who want a drink?
- When do we say "excuse me"?
- When do we say "your welcome"?
- What do we do if we want to talk to someone who is talking to someone else?
- What do we say after we burp?
- What do we do when we are sitting at the table and want something that we can't reach?
- How do we show courtesy when there are a lot of people waiting in a line to buy something at the shop and we want to buy something too?
- What do we do if our mum is busy and we say excuse me but she doesn't hear us?
- What do we say if someone lends us their toy?
- What do we say if we accidentally bump into someone?
- How do we treat peoples toys when we are in someone else's house?
- What could we do if there is someone new at school who doesn't know anyone yet?
- What do you say when when someone is using a toy that you would like to use too?

LORD OF THE ANIMALS

COURTESY STORY

The birds and the animals gathered round a wall to discuss who was to be the next lord of them all. There was shouting and yelling. No-one could hear the rest but somehow they still decided to hold a great contest.

It was to be held in a week to allow for time to practice. It would cover every element that a lord shouldn't miss. He must be strong, he must be wise, he must be good at speeches but most of all they all agreed he must be very courteous.

To test the strong they gathered weights of many different sizes. To test the wise they had a quiz to test for keen intelligence. A passage was to be read out loud for examining the best voices but what to do. How do you test for he who is most courteous.

"Excuse me," said a little mouse, "there is no way to test us, so I propose a secret vote to choose who is most courteous."
"I am wise," exclaimed the emu.
"Vote for me," giraffe asked
"I am strong," yelled hippopotamus as in the sun he basked.
And although all the animals had many kinds of qualities none seemed to be courteous. Then mouse spoke from the trees.
"Excuse me please, but if you haven't yet voted, would you very kindly vote for me instead."

The animals all went silent and each stared at the rest. Then all declared without a vote that mouse was the best. So mouse, though small, not strong and clearly not the wisest, became the lord of the animals for he won the courtesy test. Celebrations began at once. All the animals were told to come but even so they heard mouse say, "thankyou," and they all replied "Your Welcome."

MORAL – When we use our manners and are courteous people will want to listen to us.

CLEANLINESS

LESSON PLAN

DAY 1

PRAYER: Sing prayers that have been learnt and any others that the children know. Ask them to be reverent because they are talking to God.

STAR BOX: What is in the box? Soap (relate it to the story)

STORY: "Mirror Mirror"

DISCUSSION: What does cleanliness mean?
What do we do to make ourselves clean?
How do we show cleanliness before we eat our food?
Optional - Use discussion points sheet at the beginning of the book to help discuss the meaning of cleanliness.

SONG: "Wash, Wash, Wash" - sing with actions.

QUOTE:
"As soon as the mirror is cleaned and purified, the sun will manifest itself."
'Abdu'l-Bahá

Place the quotation in the letterbox as described in the beginning of the book. These are the messages God has sent us through special people. Ask a child to take out the letter.
Ask the children to say the quotation with you a couple of times. Discuss what it means.

Discussion - If a mirror is dirty then the sun can not shine its light in it. If we fill our thoughts full of horrible things there is no room for God. If our hands are grubby then only germs will grown on them and we might get sick. Being clean inside and outside helps us be and grow into the best person we can be.

ACTIVITY: Magic Mirror – Use activity sheet on the next page.
Purpose – to reflect on the virtue – to understand that being clean on the outside helps us be clean on the inside. When we are clean in and out God will be able to shine through us as virtues.

DAY 2

PRAYER: Sing prayers that have been learnt and any others that the children know. Ask them to be reverent because they are talking to God.

SONG: "Clean it up" - sing with actions.

DISCUSSION REVIEW: What does cleanliness mean?

GAME: Everyone put their hands in a container of dirt and then clean them with nice smelling soap and water. Do this with a real mirror as well. Shine a torch on it as if it is the sun. Show how you can only see the light when the mirror is clean. God will only shine through us when our thoughts are clean.
Purpose - to reflect on what it means to be clean.

QUOTE VISUALISATION:
"As soon as the mirror is cleaned and purified, the sun will manifest itself."
'Abdu'l-Bahá

Photocopy the quote visualisation page. Go through the quote with the children to help them become familiar with the words and understand the meaning. Older children may be able to memorize it. Give each child a copy of the page to colour in. Choose an activity from the front of the book to present the quotations creatively.

INSTRUCTIONS:
- Photocopy this page on to white card
- Cut out mirror
- Glue aluminium foil to back of mirror
- Colour in
- Tape a string to the back so that it can hang.

EACH CHILD WILL NEED:
- Scissors, glue, sticky tape, crayons
- White card
- Aluminium foil, a piece of string

CLEANLINESS
MAGIC MIRROR

"...AS SOON AS THE MIRROR IS CLEANED AND PURIFIED, THE SUN WILL MANIFEST ITSELF". — 'Abdu'l-Bahá

CLEANLINESS

Quote Visualisation

MIRROR MIRROR

CLEANLINESS STORY

Once upon a time their was a magic mirror which would only reflect people who were clean on the inside and clean on the outside. The mirror hung in the middle of town for everyone to see. Sari, a girl from the village, was always dirty because she played in puddles all day long, and threw vegetables when people passed by and never washed before going home. Still, she thought she would give the mirror a try. She went to it and cried the magic words,

"Mirror, mirror, mirror, shining on the stand,
what do your reflect, as I rub you with my hand."

And the mirror replied,

"Filthy on the inside, and filthy you are within,
I dare not reflect you, For you will place me in the bin."

Sari was very annoyed and decided that something had to be done. The next day after throwing some vegetables at some people walking past she went and had a bath in the river then returned to the magic mirror and spoke the words again.

"Mirror, mirror, mirror, shining on the stand,
what do your reflect, as I rub you with my hand."

And again the mirror replied but this time saying.

"Though shiny on the outside, I fear the news is bad,
your insides still are filthy, with thoughts that make me sad."

Sari became determined to see her reflection in the mirror so the next day after having another wash in the river and putting on a clean dress she stood by the side of the road and gave a flower to each person who passed. She then returned to the mirror for a third time and repeated the words.

"Mirror, mirror, mirror, shining on the stand,
what do your reflect, as I rub you with my hand."

To her joy the mirror answered, this time with these words.

"Shining on the outside, and inside you glow,
with joy I will reflect you, and show you what I know."

Then the mirror showed her her reflection and she liked what she saw and decided that this was how she wanted to be always. Clean on the inside and clean on the outside.

MORAL – Cleanliness is having a clean body and clean thoughts.

SERVICE

LESSON PLAN

DAY 1

PRAYER: Sing prayers that have been learnt and any others that the children know. Ask them to be reverent because they are talking to God.

STAR BOX: What is in the box? A magnet and some nails (relate it to the story)

STORY: "The Things Dion Needed"

DISCUSSION: What does service mean?
To be of service to someone means to do something that helps them out.
When we do a service for someone should we expect something back in return for it?
Optional - Use discussion points sheet at the beginning of the book to help discuss the meaning of service.

SONG: "Give and Take" - sing with actions

QUOTE:
"Service is the magnet which attracts the heavenly strength."
'Abdu'l-Bahá

Place the quotation in the letterbox as described in the beginning of the book. These are the messages God has sent us through special people. Ask a child to take out the letter.
Ask the children to say the quotation with you a couple of times. Discuss what it means.

Discussion - Sometimes we find it hard to do nice things but we don't always have to know everything before we start something or feel confident enough to finish it. This is because when we set out to do something nice for someone God will give us the strength and guidance to carry the task through to the end.

ACTIVITY: Fridge Magnet – Use activity sheet on the next page.
Purpose – to reflect on the virtue – to understand that by doing service we will grow and become stronger as spiritual beings. Service attracts good things to happen to us.

DAY 2

PRAYER: Sing prayers that have been learnt and any others that the children know. Ask them to be reverent because they are talking to God.

SONG: "Give and Take" - sing with actions

DISCUSSION REVIEW: What does service mean?

GAME: Someone is picked as the leader. They have to move about the room and everyone has to follow behind them. Everywhere the leader moves everyone must follow.
Purpose – to visualize how service attracts people like a magnet.

QUOTE VISUALISATION:
"Service is the magnet which attracts the heavenly strength."
'Abdu'l-Bahá

Photocopy the quote visualisation page. Go through the quote with the children to help them become familiar with the words and understand the meaning. Older children may be able to memorize it. Give each child a copy of the page to colour in. Choose an activity from the front of the book to present the quotations creatively.

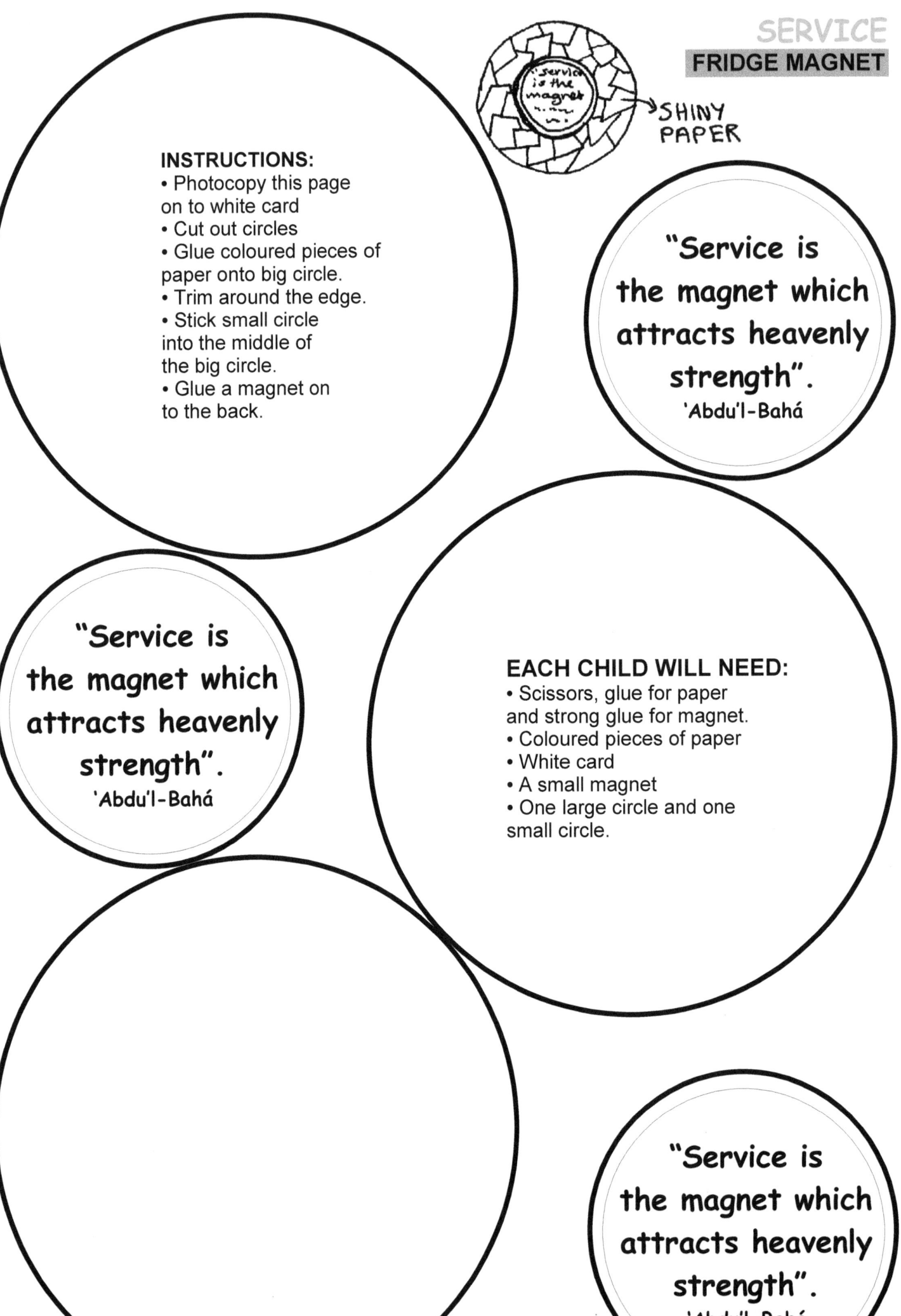

SERVICE

Quote Visualisation

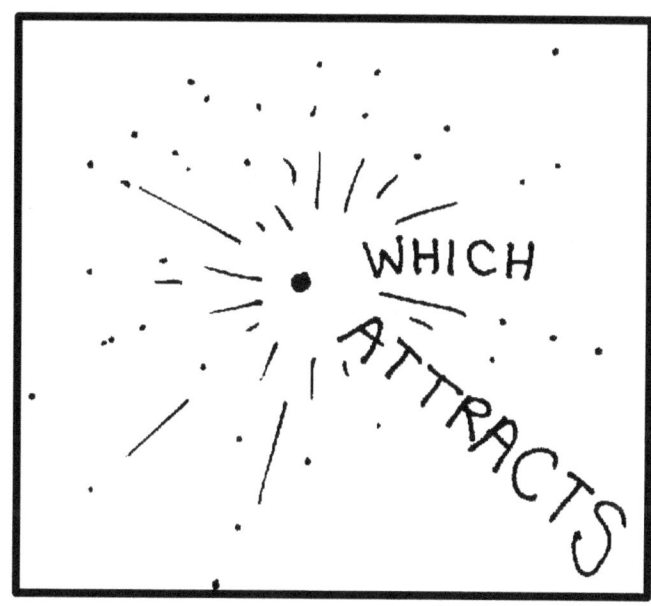

THE THINGS DION NEEDED

SERVICE STORY

Dion was sitting watching some ducks paddle in the water. He noticed that the little ducks could not swim where the river ran fast so they could not cross to the other side.
"Hmmm," thought Dion, "I wonder," he said to no-one in particular.
"Wonder what," said Betty coming up behind him.
"Oh, I was just thinking about a way for the little ducks to cross the river without being swept away by the fast flowing water." explained Dion.
"I know, a bridge," said Dion excitedly before Betty could say anything.
"But you don't know how to build a bridge," exclaimed Betty doubtfully.
Dion didn't answer because he was already running off toward home to get some things.

On the way he met farmer Jack.
"What are you in such a hurry for?" said farmer Jack.
"I'm going to build a bridge so the little ducks can get across the river," explained Dion.
"You don't know how to build a bridge, I'D better bring some wood down and help you." called farmer Jack as Dion ran off.

He ran so fast that he bumped into Ralph from the hardware store.
"Careful, you nearly knocked me over. Where are you off to anyway?" asked Ralph suspiciously.
"I'm going to build a bridge so the little ducks can get across the river," explained Dion again.
"Bridges are tricky things to build. I'll bring down some nails and give you a hand," called Ralph as Dion disappeared around a corner.

He was nearly home when he passed his neighbor, Tommy.
"Hey Dion, what are you doing?"
"I'm going to build a bridge so the little ducks can get across the river," explained Dion for the third time.
"You can't just build a bridge, you need a plan. I'll draw one up and bring it down for you."
"Thanks," replied Dion as he leaped through the door of his house.

SERVICE STORY

"Mum, Mum, I need some rope." shouted Dion breathlessly.
"Whatever for?" Asked Dion's mum coming out of the kitchen with flour on her hands.
"I'm going to build a bridge so the little ducks can get across the river," explained Dion once again.
"Well the rope is in the shed. I'll bring down some lemonade and cake." stated Mum.
Dion grabbed the rope and sped back down to the river.

Tommy was already there finishing his plan and farmer Jack had just arrived carrying some wood.
Ralph arrived next with the nails and tools so they set about following Tommy's plan for the bridge.
Dion tied his rope on and by the time they were finished Dion's mum had arrived with morning tea for everyone.

They sat on the river, admired their work and ate and drank while the mother duck led her Bábies over their new bridge.
Betty sat by amazed, "Wow, I really didn't think you could do it."
"Neither did I really," pondered Dion, "It was all the help I picked up on the way that made it all turn out right."

MORAL – When we set out to do service with good intentions, we don't need everything in the beginning because we can pick up the things we need along the way, like a magnet.

DETACHMENT

LESSON PLAN

DAY 1

PRAYER: Sing prayers that have been learnt and any others that the children know. Ask them to be reverent because they are talking to God.

STAR BOX: What is in the box? A feather (relate it to the story)

STORY: "The Biggest of Birds"

DISCUSSION: What does detachment mean?
Detachment means to let go of something.
When we give a gift to someone we should give it to them with our heart and not think of wanting it back again.
How could we be datached if something special to us was accidentally broken?
Optional - Use discussion points sheet at the beginning of the book to help discuss the meaning of detachment.

SONG: "Let Go" - sing with actions

QUOTE:
"Cast away that which ye possess, and , on the wings of detachment, soar beyond all created things."
    Bahá'u'lláh

Place the quotation in the letterbox as described in the beginning of the book. These are the messages God has sent us through special people. Ask a child to take out the letter.
Ask the children to say the quotation with you a couple of times. Discuss what it means.

Discussion - Don't be attached to material things like clothes, toys, cars, food etc...
These things fade away, get broken, get old, get lost in time and are not really what is most important. Focus on being a person who gives and shares and be detached from all these things that surround us each day.

ACTIVITY: Wings of detachment – Use activity sheet on the next page.
Purpose – to visualize the quotation – to understand that being detached frees you from all material things.

DAY 2

PRAYER: Sing prayers that have been learnt and any others that the children know. Ask them to be reverent because they are talking to God.

SONG: "Let Go" - sing with actions

DISCUSSION REVIEW: What does detachment mean?

GAME: Each person has a turn at being blindfolded while another carefully leads them about.
Purpose – to practice letting go of, being detached from, the things that we know

QUOTE VISUALISATION:
"Cast away that which ye possess, and , on the wings of detachment, soar beyond all created things."
    Bahá'u'lláh

Photocopy the quote visualisation page. Go through the quote with the children to help them become familiar with the words and understand the meaning. Older children may be able to memorize it. Give each child a copy of the page to colour in. Choose an activity from the front of the book to present the quotations creatively.

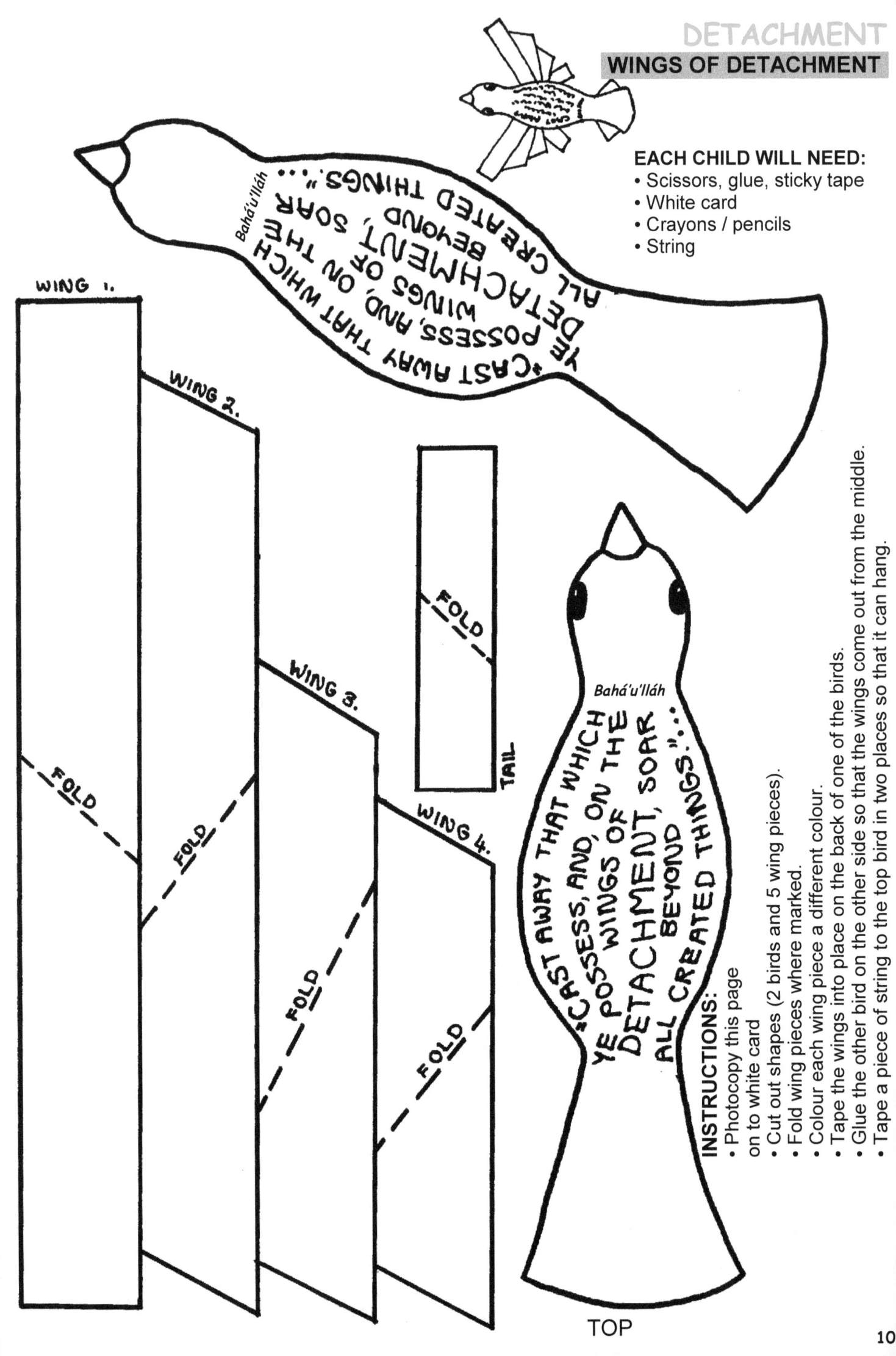

Quote Visualisation

DETACHMENT

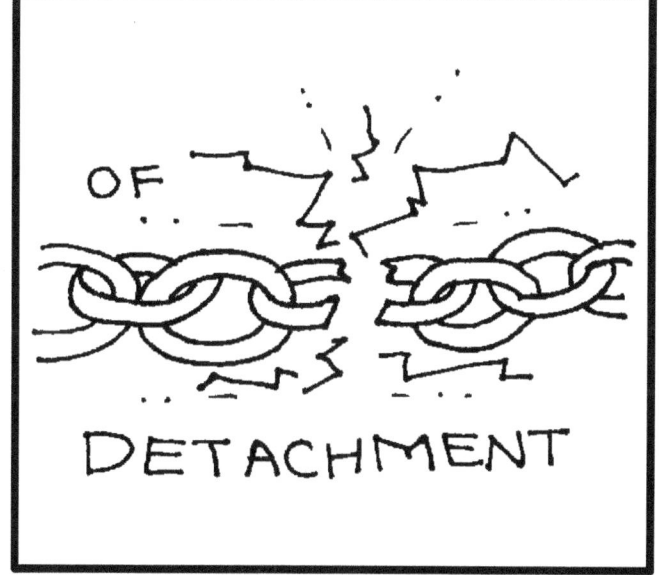

THE BIGGEST OF BIRDS

DETACHMENT STORY

Maisy was a little bird who wanted to be a very big bird. When all her brothers and sisters learnt to fly and left the nest to make their own homes Maisy was still hopping around on the ground trying to look big. She was determined to have the biggest tail, the most colourful feathers, the largest beak and the longest wings. She found big peacock feathers to add to her tail. She found some left over paint to colour her feathers like the rainbow. She held a stick in her beak to make it look larger and added some crow's feathers to make her wings longer. By the time she was finished, she looked ridiculous.

She strutted about saying "I am so big, the biggest of birds, the most extra-ordinary feathered creature."
Her brothers and sisters looked down from the sky and called to her loudly. "You look very small to us from up here in the sky."
Maisy looked up at them enviously and decided this just wasn't right. She was big, not small. She had to learn to fly.

DETACHMENT
STORY

She waddled to a cliff top, took a run up and jumped as far as she could into the air. For a moment she felt wonderful and then she started to fall down, down, down until.... plop. She fell hard onto the ground. She got up limping and very sore. Again and again she tried but always she fell to the ground.

She looked at her added feathers and paint. Then she looked at her brothers and sisters high in the sky. They can fly with their small tail and wings but I cannot fly at all with my large ones. She was miserable all the next day until finally she took off the extra feathers, let go of the stick in her mouth and washed the paint off in the pond.

Then she climbed to the top of the cliff again. Took a deep breath, spread her wings and leaped as far as she could with her eyes closed. For a moment she fell and then an amazing feeling came over her. She opened her eyes and saw the ground far below her. The wind ruffled her feathers as she flew higher and higher. She felt so big, so extra-ordinary, so fantastic. She left her added feathers and her paint and the ground below far behind her and never looked back. She soared and twirled and felt the wind ripple her feathers. As she flew she thought about how much better this was than any silly feathers and paint.

MORAL – Detachment means to let go of the things that tie you down in order that your spirit can soar high in the sky.

JOYFULNESS

LESSON PLAN

DAY 1

PRAYER: Sing prayers that have been learnt and any others that the children know. Ask them to be reverent because they are talking to God.

STAR BOX: What is in the box? A balloon (relate it to the story)

STORY: "Happy to be Blue"

DISCUSSION: What does joyfulness mean?
Joyfulness means to be happy.
What is something that makes you feel joyful?
When you are happy that can make other people feel happy to.
Optional - Use discussion points sheet at the beginning of the book to help discuss the meaning of joyfulness.

SONG: "In My Heart" - sing with actions.

QUOTE:
"Turn all your thoughts toward bringing joy to hearts"
'Abdu'l-Bahá
Place the quotation in the letterbox as described in the beginning of the book. These are the messages God has sent us through special people. Ask a child to take out the letter.
Ask the children to say the quotation with you a couple of times. Discuss what it means.

Discussion - Concentrate and focus your energy on making other people sad. Say and do things that bring joy instead of saddness.

ACTIVITY: Spinning Joy – Use activity sheet on the next page.
Purpose – to visualize the quotation – to understand that wherever we turn and whoever we come across we should strive to bring them joy and happiness.

DAY 2

PRAYER: Sing prayers that have been learnt and any others that the children know. Ask them to be reverent because they are talking to God.

SONG: "In My Heart" - sing with actions.

DISCUSSION REVIEW: What does joyfulness mean?

GAME: Each person has a turn at putting marshmallows into their mouth one at a time. After each marshmallow they have to say "I bring joy to hearts" When their mouth is so full that they cannot say the words anymore then they have to stop.
Purpose – to be joyful.

QUOTE VISUALISATION:
"Turn all your thoughts toward bringing joy to hearts"
'Abdu'l-Bahá
Photocopy the quote visualisation page. Go through the quote with the children to help them become familiar with the words and understand the meaning. Older children may be able to memorize it. Give each child a copy of the page to colour in. Choose an activity from the front of the book to present the quotations creatively.

JOYFULNESS
SPINNING JOY

INSTRUCTIONS:
• Photocopy this page on to coloured card
• Cut out the two shapes
• Cut square where marked
• Fold square where marked
• Join circle and square together through the centre with a paper fastner.
• Tape a popstick on to the back.

EACH CHILD WILL NEED:
• Scissors, sticky tape
• A copy of this page on coloured card
• A popstick
• A paper fastner

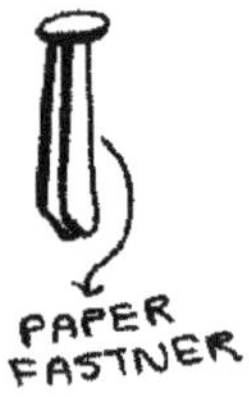

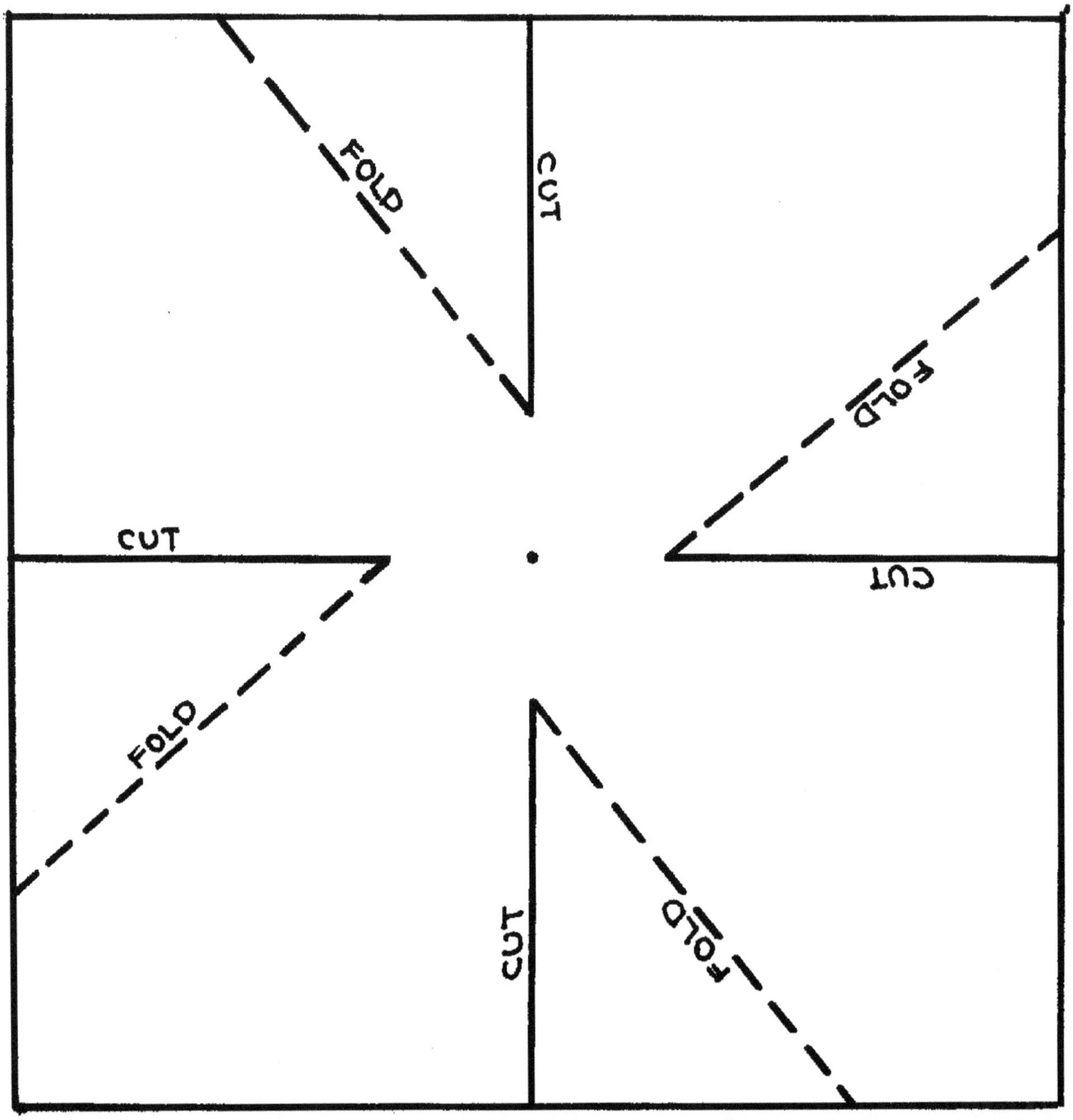

Quote Visualisation — JOYFULNESS

HAPPY TO BE BLUE

JOYFULNESS STORY

It was party time and all the balloons were ecstatically happy. As always, when they were this happy, they blew up big and round and floated to the top of the ceiling making the room look beautiful and colourful ready for the party. Benny balloon though was always feeling blue because that was his colour. Unfortunately feeling blue was the same as feeling miserable so he always remained kind of flat and never floated to the ceiling. He rolled about on the floor moaning, "stop all that noise, it's just a party" and "I don't see what all the excitement is about."

The problem was, this party was Bobby's party and his favorite colour was blue. The balloons did not want to let Bobby down by having no blue balloons. "We must cheer Benny balloon up," they all agreed. They tickled him, they said funny jokes and they played hide and seek but nothing worked. Benny was as miserable as ever. In fact, he even started crying. "This is no good," the other balloons groaned.

"I have an idea," squeaked Rosy the red balloon who was always feeling especially bright and cheery because that was her colour. "Let's tell him how much he means to Bobby, it might make him feel important."

They all liked to feel important so they gave it a go. At first it didn't seem to work. Then Benny the balloon who was always feeling blue started to smile. Then Benny the ballloon who was always feeling down started to rise up. Then Benny the balloon who was always on the bottom rose to the very top.

"Hurray," cried all the balloons just before all Bobby's friends arrived for the happiest blue party ever.

MORAL – Joy gives us the energy to live life to the fullest.

THOUGHTFULNESS

LESSON PLAN

DAY 1

PRAYER: Sing prayers that have been learnt and any others that the children know. Ask them to be reverent because they are talking to God.

STAR BOX: What is in the box? - A small box or fake jewels (relate it to the story)

STORY: "Inside, Outside"

DISCUSSION: What does thoughtfulness mean?
Being thoughtful of others means to think about other peoples needs and feelings.
If someone forgets to bring the pencils to school and you have lot's how could you show that you are being thoughtful?
Optional - Use discussion points sheet at the beginning of the book to help discuss the meaning of thoughtfulness.

SONG: "The Inside" - sing with actions

QUOTE:
"The reality of man is his thought, not his material body."
'Abdu'l-Bahá
Place the quotation in the letterbox as described in the beginning of the book. These are the messages God has sent us through special people. Ask a child to take out the letter.
Ask the children to say the quotation with you a couple of times. Discuss what it means.

Discussion - Although we can see only body, our arms, legs, toes etc... This is not really what makes us special. It is the thoughts we carry inside us that make us who we are.

ACTIVITY: Thoughtful window decorations – Use activity sheet on the next page.
Purpose – to reflect on the quotation – to understand that our true reality is inside us. It is our that our thoughts are a reflection of who we really are.

DAY 2

PRAYER: Sing prayers that have been learnt and any others that the children know. Ask them to be reverent because they are talking to God.

SONG: "The Inside" - sing with actions

DISCUSSION REVIEW: What does thoughtfulness mean?

GAME: Each person has a turn at thinking of a virtue. They try to mime it out while the others try to guess what the virtue is.
Purpose – to practice expressing thoughts.

QUOTE VISUALISATION:
"The reality of man is his thought, not his material body."
'Abdu'l-Bahá
Photocopy the quote visualisation page. Go through the quote with the children to help them become familiar with the words and understand the meaning. Older children may be able to memorize it. Give each child a copy of the page to colour in. Choose an activity from the front of the book to present the quotations creatively.

THOUGHTFULNESS
THOUGHTFUL WINDOW DECORATIONS

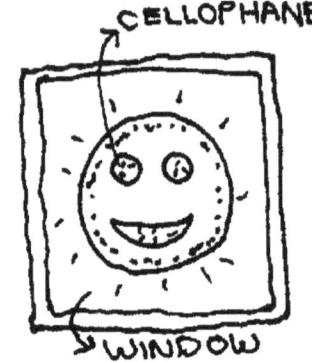

EACH CHILD WILL NEED:
- Scissors, glue
- A copy of a face
- A piece of cellophane
- Bluetack

INSTRUCTIONS:
- Photocopy this page on to coloured card
- Cut out the circle
- Glue a piece of cellophane on to the back.
- Trim off excess cellophane
- Use bluetack to stick it to a window and watch the light shine through it like our thoughts shine through us.

Quote Visualisation

THOUGHTFULNESS

INSIDE, OUTSIDE

THOUGHTFULNESS
STORY

On an ordinary shelf in an ordinary shop sat two boxes. One was beautiful with colourful decorations, but the other was plain and ugly. The beautiful box was very proud of its lovely colours and would chatter away to the ugly box about how the first customer that walks into the shop would pick him out as the most unique, most wonderful piece of work and buy him immediately.

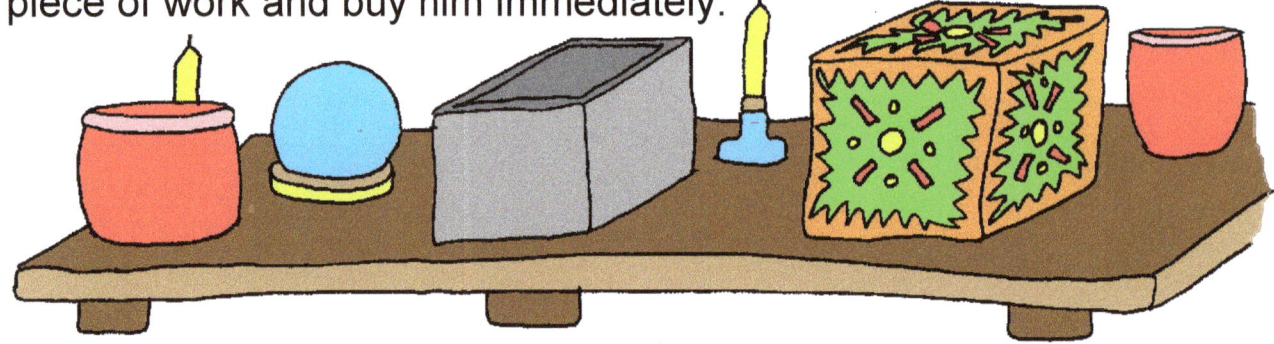

It wasn't long before a lady came into the shop looking for a special gift for a special friend. The beautiful box smiled confidently and muttered about how it would only be a matter of time before he was noticed. The lady did notice the beautiful box and opened its lid to look inside, but there was nothing in there. Then she closed the lid and started to walk away. The beautiful box could not believe it. He was the most beautiful, most wonderful thing in the shop, wasn't he?

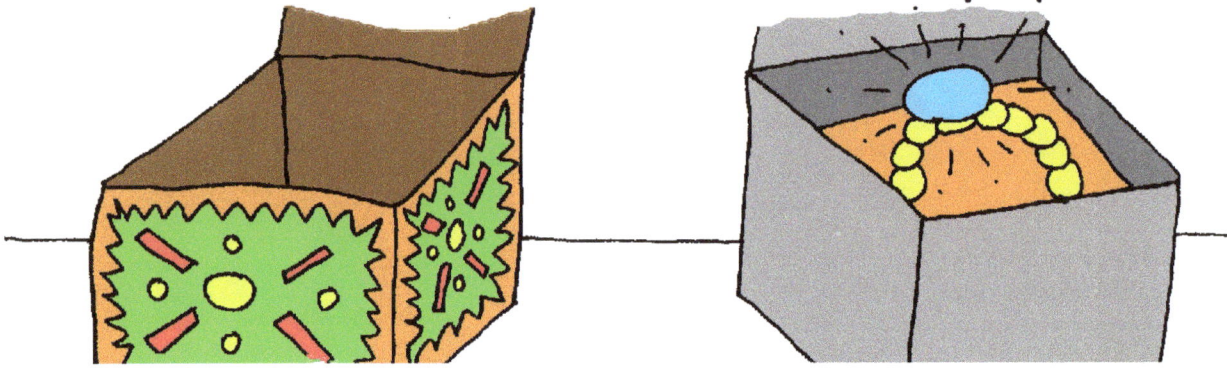

Just as the lady was leaving she suddenly spied the ugly box and walked over to take a look. She opened the lid and peeped inside, A brilliant smile lit up her face. Inside was a beautiful shiny necklace. She closed the box and bought it immediately. The beautiful box never again boasted about his beautiful decorative outside because he now realized it was what was inside that counted most.

MORAL – The thoughts inside us are more important than our outside appearance.

HUMILITY

LESSON PLAN

DAY 1

PRAYER: Sing prayers that have been learnt and any others that the children know. Ask them to be reverent because they are talking to God.

STAR BOX: What is in the box? - A child's cup from a teaset - a thimble or small lid could do instead (relate it to the story)

STORY: "Fill Her Up"

DISCUSSION: What does Humility mean?
Being humble means that you always remember that you have many things to learn and don't pretend that you know everything.
How could we show humility when our teacher is explaining something to us?
Optional - Use discussion points sheet at the beginning of the book to help discuss the meaning of humility.

SONG: "Humility" - sing with actions.

QUOTE: *"My dominion is my humility"*
   'Abdu'l-Bahá

Place the quotation in the letterbox as described in the beginning of the book. These are the messages God has sent us through special people. Ask a child to take out the letter.
Ask the children to say the quotation with you a couple of times. Discuss what it means.

Humility makes us stronger spiritually. When we are humble we can respect other people, learn from other people and become a better person. Arrogance and pride stops us growing and in the end makes us weaker.

ACTIVITY: Humility cups – Use activity sheet on the next page.
Purpose – to reflect on the quotation – to understand that our greatness lies in our ability to humble ourselves and let God work though us. Because only with God's help can we reach our true potential.

DAY 2

PRAYER: Sing prayers that have been learnt and any others that the children know. Ask them to be reverent because they are talking to God.

SONG: "Humility" - sing with actions.

DISCUSSION REVIEW: What does Humility mean?

GAME: Hold a stick about a meter and a half off the ground. Everyone has to line up and go under it by bending backwards. The stick is then lowered and the same thing happens. The stick is then lowered again and again etc... If someone can't do it they sit out to the end of the game. The person who lasts the longest wins the game.
Purpose - to visualize how being the lowest or most humble wins in the end.

QUOTE VISUALISATION: *"My dominion is my humility"*
   'Abdu'l-Bahá

Photocopy the quote visualisation page. Go through the quote with the children to help them become familiar with the words and understand the meaning. Older children may be able to memorize it. Give each child a copy of the page to colour in. Choose an activity from the front of the book to present the quotations creatively.

HUMILITY
HUMILITY CUPS

"My dominion is my humility"
'Abdu'l-Bahá

"My dominion is my humility"
'Abdu'l-Bahá

"My dominion is my humility"
'Abdu'l-Bahá

"My dominion is my humility"
'Abdu'l-Bahá

"My dominion is my humility"
'Abdu'l-Bahá

"My dominion is my humility"
'Abdu'l-Bahá

PLASTIC CUP
COLOURED PIECES OF PAPER
QUOTATION

"My dominion is my humility"
'Abdu'l-Bahá

"My dominion is my humility"
'Abdu'l-Bahá

"My dominion is my humility"
'Abdu'l-Bahá

"My dominion is my humility"
'Abdu'l-Bahá

INSTRUCTIONS:
- Photocopy this page on to white card
- Cut out the quotations
- Glue coloured pieces of paper around the cup
- Glue the quotations on to the cup.

EACH CHILD WILL NEED:
- Scissors, strong glue
- A copy of a quotation
- Small pieces of coloured paper
- A plastic cup

HUMILITY

Quote Visualisation

FILL HER UP

HUMILITY
STORY

The table was ready and the guests were just arriving. Some new cups had been unpacked especially for this occasion, a birthday party. Cathy cup was watching all the people in their lovely dresses and jackets. Peter was sitting next to her and suddenly said,
"I can't wait to be filled up with some yummy fruit punch."
"I'm not going to let anyone fill me up with anything. I am nice and clean and I am going to stay like that." stated Cathy, horrified at the very thought.

Just then Cathy felt herself being lifted from the table. Someone pored juice into her, or at least they tried to. Cathy squinted up her eyes and breathed in very tightly so that the juice went everywhere except inside her. The person holding the cup exclaimed,
"This one must have a leak."
Then to Cathy's dismay she was tossed into the rubbish bin.

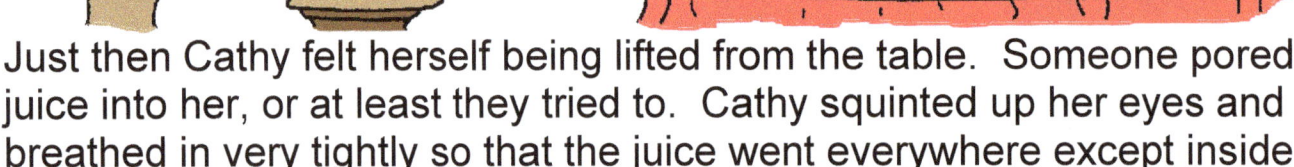

Later that night the garbage was taken out and placed at the edge of the road ready for the rubbish truck. Cathy was dumped with broken pieces, old tissues, dirty paper plates and rotten food. She squinted her eyes and held her breath, this time to keep the smell out. She lay in the hot sun and wondered what would happen to her next. She was now far more dirty than if she just had juice in her.

A few days later a homeless man came looking through the rubbish. He soon spied Cathy and picked her up with glee. He took out an old rag from his pocket and rubbed until she was shining again. Cathy shone back at him feeling very grateful and much better. That night when the homeless man filled her at a spring with water she willingly let herself be filled up and proudly let him drink from her.

MORAL – Humility is knowing that we are nothing on our own. When we let ourselves be used for God's purpose we become something special.

PATIENCE

LESSON PLAN

DAY 1

PRAYER: Sing prayers that have been learnt and any others that the children know. Ask them to be reverent because they are talking to God.

STAR BOX: What is in the box? A clock / watch (relate it to the story)

STORY: "I Just Can't Wait"

DISCUSSION: What does patience mean?
Patience means waiting quietly for something without complaining.
How can we show our patience when our mum is getting some food for us and we are feeling very hungry?
Optional - Use discussion points sheet at the beginning of the book to help discuss the meaning of patience.

SONG: "Be Patient" - sing with actions.

QUOTE:
"Be patient under all conditions"
    Bahá'u'lláh
Place the quotation in the letterbox as described in the beginning of the book. These are the messages God has sent us through special people. Ask a child to take out the letter.
Ask the children to say the quotation with you a couple of times. Discuss what it means.

Discussion - It doesn't matter if there is rain, sun, thunder we still need to be patient. I doesn't matter if we want something to happen quickly or we want something to finish quickly. Whatever the situation we are in we still need to be patient.

ACTIVITY: Patient Clock – Use activity sheet on the next page.
Purpose – to reflect on the virtue – to understand that everything has a time to happen. If you wait you will see results.

DAY 2

PRAYER: Sing prayers that have been learnt and any others that the children know. Ask them to be reverent because they are talking to God.

SONG: "Crown of Jewels" - sing with actions.

DISCUSSION REVIEW: What does patience mean?

GAME: Divide group into pairs. Each pair stares into each others eyes patiently. The winner is the one who can stare without blinking for the longest.
Purpose - to practice patience.

QUOTE VISUALISATION:
"Be patient under all conditions"
    Bahá'u'lláh
Photocopy the quote visualisation page. Go through the quote with the children to help them become familiar with the words and understand the meaning. Older children may be able to memorize it. Give each child a copy of the page to colour in. Choose an activity from the front of the book to present the quotations creatively.

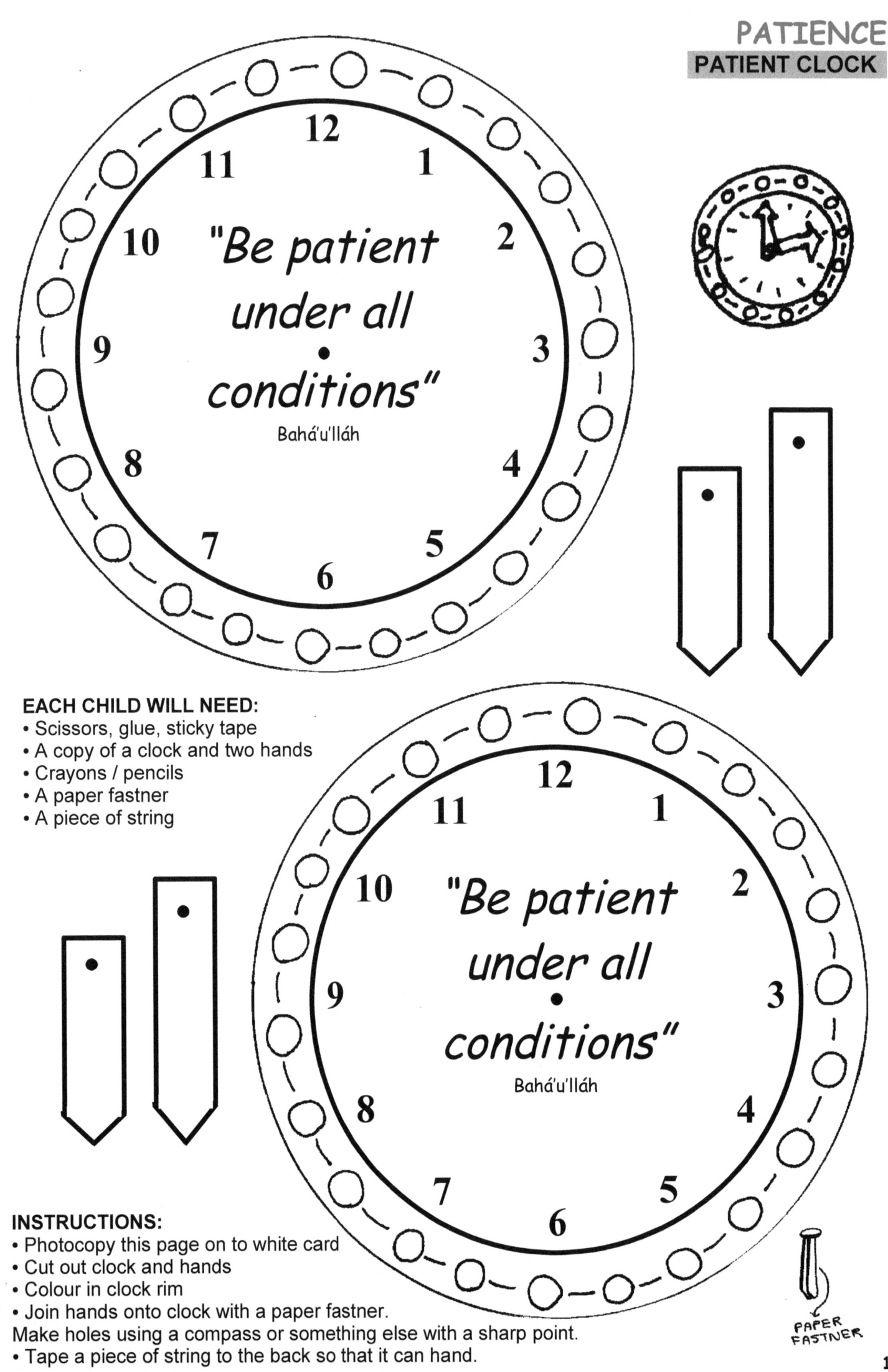

Quote Visualisation   PATIENCE

I JUST CAN'T WAIT

PATIENCE
STORY

Lucy wanted to play with her ball.
"I just can't wait," she said with a sigh.
But it was raining outside so she sat down to read a book instead and patiently wait.

"I just can't wait," exclaimed Lucy.
But it didn't stop raining. Instead lightning and thunder roared in the sky. It had turned into a big thunderstorm. So she sat down and played with some blocks and patiently waited.

"I just can't wait," said Lucy looking out the window to check the sky. The sun was shining and who was driving up to the house but her cousin Hilda.
"Hilda, do you want to play with my ball," said Lucy excitedly.
"No, I'm tired. Let's do a puzzle instead." said Hilda.
Lucy sighed and went to get a puzzle.

After the puzzle she and Hilda were heading for the door to play with the ball. Lucy could not contain her excitement, she jumped up and down with joy. Just as her hand touched the door knob mum called, "Lucy, Hilda, time for afternoon tea."
"Oh no," Lucy complained, "Not again."

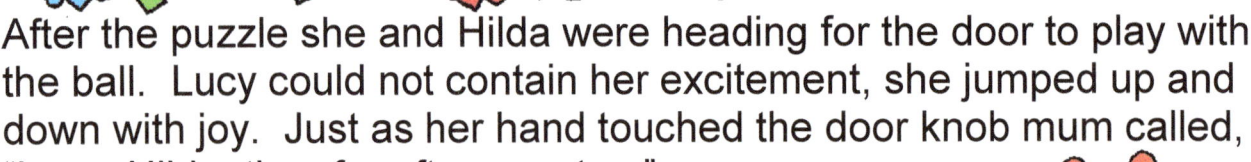

After afternoon tea Lucy and Hilda again headed for the door.
"Lucy," called mum again.
Lucy was getting a bit frustrated now, being patient was very hard.
"Here's two batts for you to use with your ball," stated mum.
"Oh wow," cried Lucy very relieved and happy.
They had a lovely game and played until it got dark. Afterwards Lucy thought about the day and decided that it was so much fun that all that waiting patiently was really worth it.

MORAL – Good things come to those who wait patiently.

PERSEVERANCE

LESSON PLAN

DAY 1

PRAYER: Sing prayers that have been learnt and any others that the children know. Ask them to be reverent because they are talking to God.

STAR BOX: What is in the box? A matchbox car (relate it to the story)

STORY: "Tiny Timmy"

DISCUSSION: What does perseverance mean?
Perseverance means to keep trying even when something is difficult.
How can we persevere when we are running in a race?
Optional - Use discussion points sheet at the beginning of the book to help discuss the meaning of perseverance.

SONG: "Don't Stop" - sing with actions

QUOTE:
"Victories are won usually through... perseverance, and rarely accomplished at a single stroke."
From a letter written on behalf of Shoghi Effendi
Place the quotation in the letterbox as described in the beginning of the book. These are the messages God has sent us through special people. Ask a child to take out the letter.
Ask the children to say the quotation with you a couple of times. Discuss what it means.

Discussion - A picture is not coloured by just one stroke of a pencil it is accomplished through careful colouring all across the page. A race is not won in one step but by sweating and puffing all the way to the finish line. We do not achieve success straight away but only from continually trying and persevering.

ACTIVITY: Trophy – Use activity sheet on the next page.
Purpose – to visualize the quotation – to reflect on how effort equals achievement.

DAY 2

PRAYER: Sing prayers that have been learnt and any others that the children know. Ask them to be reverent because they are talking to God.

SONG: "Don't Stop" - sing with actions

DISCUSSION REVIEW: What does perseverance mean?

GAME: See how many popsticks each person can pile on top of each other before it falls down.
Purpose - to practice perseverance.

QUOTE VISUALISATION:
"Victories are won usually through... perseverance, and rarely accomplished at a single stroke."
From a letter written on behalf of Shoghi Effendi
Photocopy the quote visualisation page. Go through the quote with the children to help them become familiar with the words and understand the meaning. Older children may be able to memorize it. Give each child a copy of the page to colour in. Choose an activity from the front of the book to present the quotations creatively.

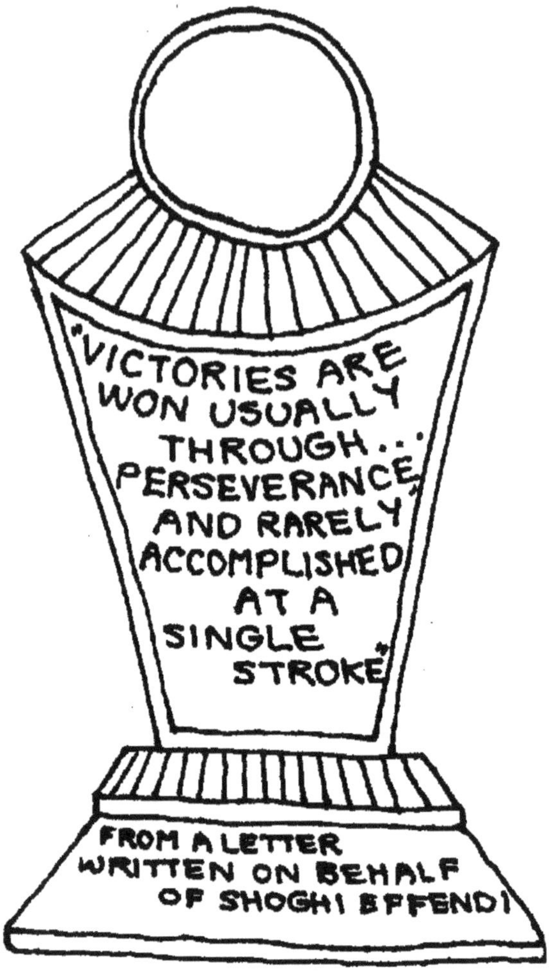

PERSEVERANCE TROPHY

"VICTORIES ARE WON USUALLY THROUGH... PERSEVERANCE, AND RARELY ACCOMPLISHED AT A SINGLE STROKE"

FROM A LETTER WRITTEN ON BEHALF OF SHOGHI EFFENDI

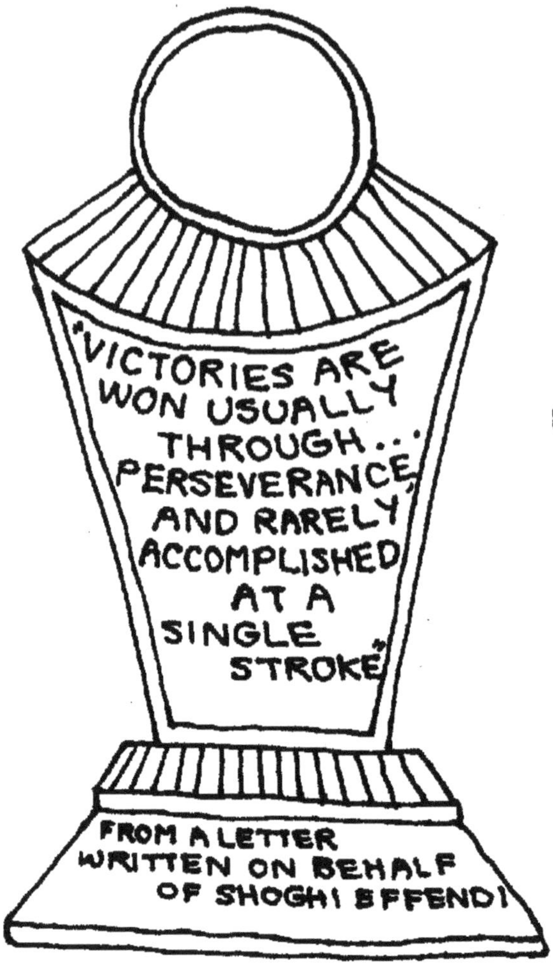

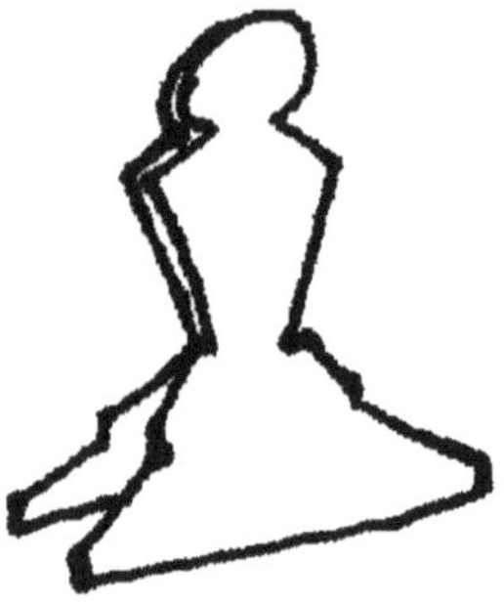

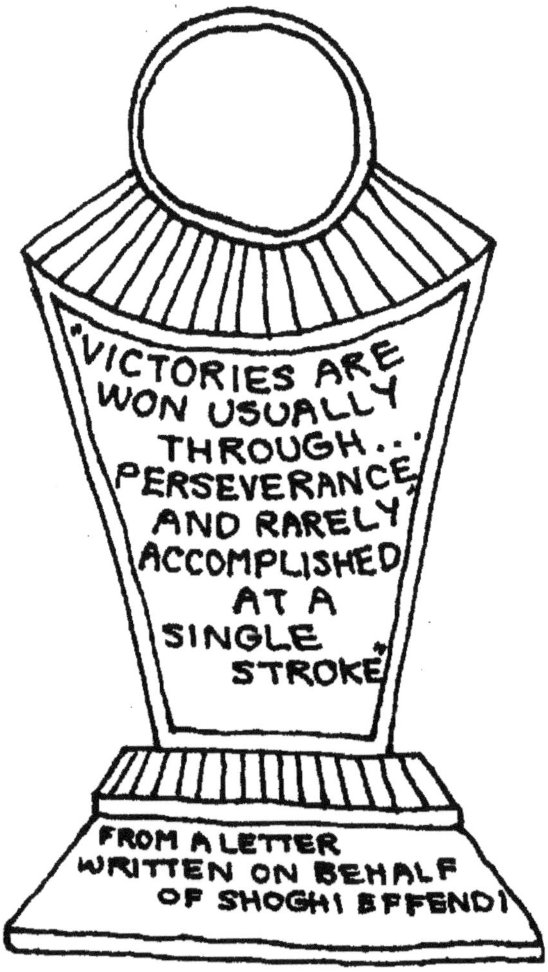

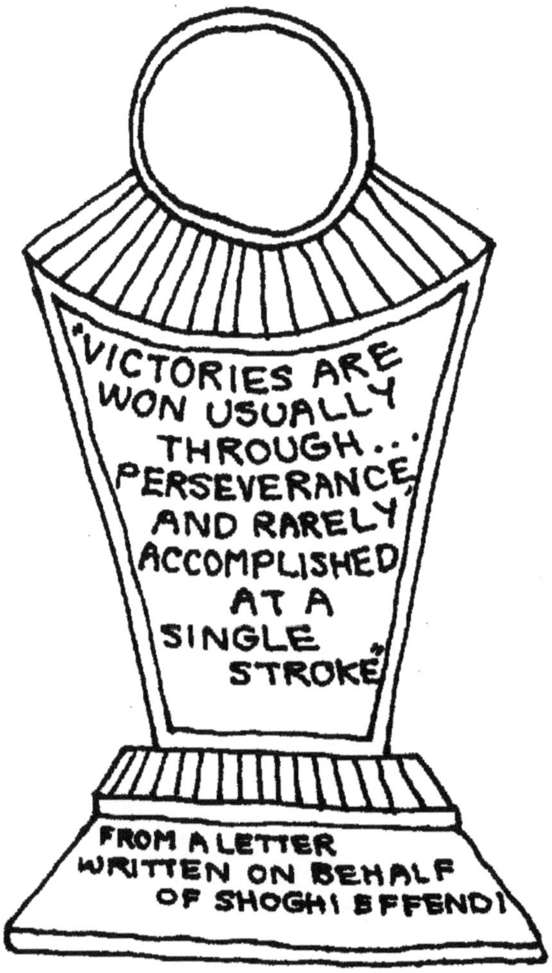

EACH CHILD WILL NEED:
- Scissors, glue
- A copy of two trophies on to white card
- Glitter pen
- Crayons / pencils

INSTRUCTIONS:
- Photocopy this page on to white card
- Cut out two trophies
- Stick them back to back with the bottom part unglued.
- Colour in
- Use a glitter pen on the circle at the top.
- Fold the bottom parts out so that it will stand.

Quote Visualisation PERSEVERANCE

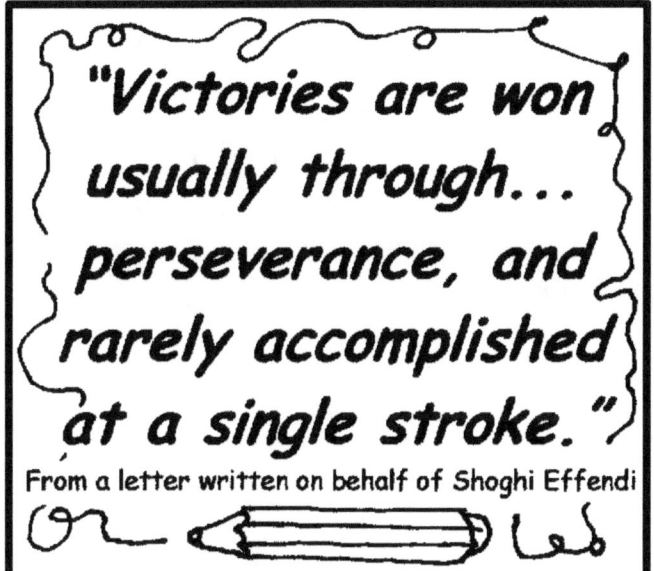

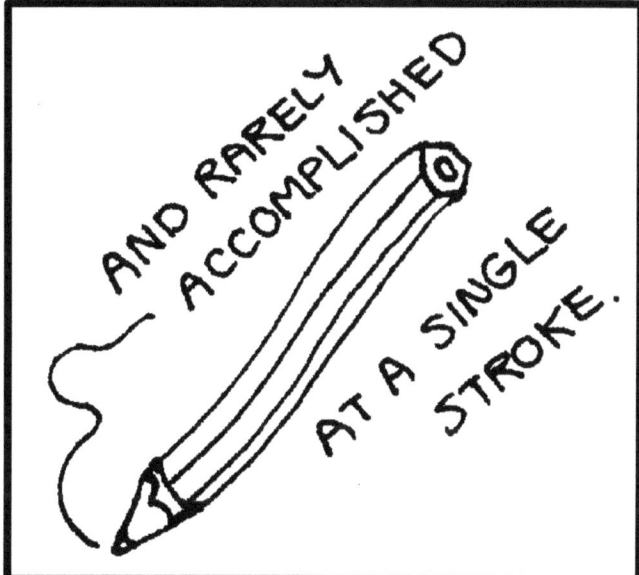

TINY TIMMY

PERSEVERANCE STORY

Barry, the biggest tyre in the shop was on the lookout for any cars who needed new tyres. It had been a busy day and he was enjoying a few minutes of silence.
"Excuse me" said a voice in an important tone.
"Do you have a spare tyre, I have a hole in my front wheel and I am in a big hurry to deliver a special birthday package."
"Well, you have come to the right place." said Barry.
"I'll see what we have in the shop."
He disappeared into the shop for a moment and to his dismay the place was nearly empty. It really had been a busy day. The only tyre left was Timmy the tiniest tyre they had.
"I can do the job," he squeaked confidently.
"Well, I don't know," said Barry uncertainly.
"I won't let you down," squeaked Timmy as he rolled through the door without waiting for an answer. By the time Barry had got outside again, Timmy was already attatched to the car which was tooting a goodbye and heading off down the road. Timmy smiled to himself.
He was on his first job. He was clean and shiny and ready for anything, or so he thought.

It was easy at first, just rolling along, but then it started to get bumpy. Rocks were scattered along the road. There were times when he thought he would come right off his axle. Then they came to some water. He had to take a deep breath and hold it in for a long time until they got to the other side. He came out gasping for breath but there was no time for resting because the car was speeding off again.

The next thing they came to was mud. It was slippery and slimy and it took all Timmy's strength and determination to keep the car on the road. The road finally became smooth again and they came to rest outside a farm house. A lady ran out and took a package from the car.
"Thank you so much," she said, "Lilly would have been so disappointed if she didn't get any presents for her birthday. You saved the day."
Timmy smiled, still gasping for breath. He had done it, and what a special job it was too. He felt like a hero as the car slowly drove back down the road.

MORAL – Perseverance is not giving up when things get hard.

RESPONSIBILITY

LESSON PLAN

DAY 1

PRAYER: Sing prayers that have been learnt and any others that the children know. Ask them to be reverent because they are talking to God.

BOX: What is in the box? A strawberry or small plant (relate it to the story)

STAR STORY: "Fiona's Frustration"

DISCUSSION: What does responsibility mean?
When we are responsible we know that we have to do our share of the work, look after things that we are trusted with and not let other people take the blame for something that was our fault. How can we be responsible for our toys?
Optional - Use discussion points sheet at the beginning of the book to help discuss the meaning of responsibility.

SONG: "I Am Responsible" - sing with actions

QUOTE:
"Each human creature has individual... responsibility in the creative plan of God."
    'Abdu'l-Bahá
Place the quotation in the letterbox as described in the beginning of the book. These are the messages God has sent us through special people. Ask a child to take out the letter.
Ask the children to say the quotation with you a couple of times. Discuss what it means.

Discussion - God has a plan and purpose for all of us, whether we are a grain of dirt, a flower, an animal or a person. We are responsible for doing a part in the best way we can.

ACTIVITY: Flower Pot – Use activity sheet on the next page.
Purpose – to practice the virtue – to understand that being responsible is a rewarding action.

DAY 2

PRAYER: Sing prayers that have been learnt and any others that the children know. Ask them to be reverent because they are talking to God.

SONG: "I Am Responsible" - sing with actions

DISCUSSION REVIEW: What does responsibility mean?

GAME: Use a simple jigsaw and give each child at least one piece each. Each child is responsible for putting their pieces into the puzzle.
Purpose – for everyone to be responsible for a small part of the 'bigger picture'

QUOTE VISUALISATION:
"Each human creature has individual... responsibility in the creative plan of God."
    'Abdu'l-Bahá
Photocopy the quote visualisation page. Go through the quote with the children to help them become familiar with the words and understand the meaning. Older children may be able to memorize it. Give each child a copy of the page to colour in. Choose an activity from the front of the book to present the quotations creatively.

RESPONSIBILITY
FLOWER POT

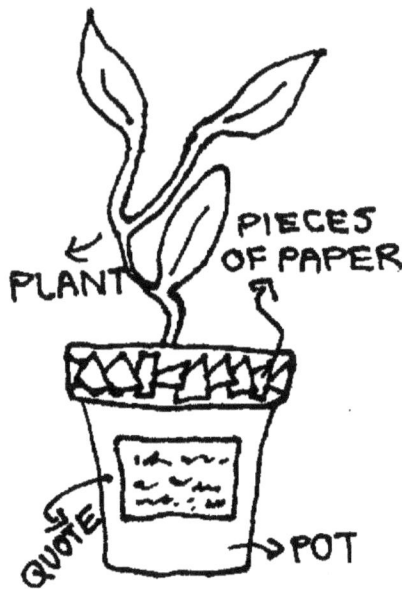

"Each human creature
has individual...
responsibility
in the creative plan
of God."
'Abdu'l-Bahá

"Each human creature
has individual...
responsibility
in the creative plan
of God."
'Abdu'l-Bahá

"Each human creature
has individual...
responsibility
in the creative plan
of God."
'Abdu'l-Bahá

"Each human creature
has individual...
responsibility
in the creative plan
of God."
'Abdu'l-Bahá

"Each human creature
has individual...
responsibility
in the creative plan
of God."
'Abdu'l-Bahá

"Each human creature
has individual...
responsibility
in the creative plan
of God."
'Abdu'l-Bahá

"Each human creature
has individual...
responsibility
in the creative plan
of God."
'Abdu'l-Bahá

INSTRUCTIONS:
- Photocopy this page on to white card
- Cut out the quotations
- Glue the quotations on to the flower pot (plastic cups could or old containers could be used instead)
- Glue coloured pieces of paper around the rim of the flower pot.
- Plant a small seedling in the pot.
- Children take it home and practice being responsible by taking care of it and watering it.

RESPONSIBILITY

Quote Visualisation

FIONA'S FRUSTRATION

RESPONSIBILITY STORY

"I want a pet, I want a pet," demanded Fiona crossly.
"It takes a lot of responsibility to have a pet," replied Aunt Sophy calmly.
"I want a pet, I want a pet," demanded Fiona again.
"I know," said Aunt Sophy after thinking for a while. "We will get you a plant to see if you are responsible enough to have a pet."
"I don't want a plant, I want a pet," exclaimed a very cross Fiona.
Aunt Sophy ignored her ranting and raving and the next day when she woke up she found a little seedling at the end of her bed. Poking out of the soil was a note that read;

'When the plant is grown you will have your pet.'

Fiona cried a few frustrated tears. Most people gave her everything she wanted but Aunt Sophy didn't.

"I don't know how to look after a plant," moaned Fiona to herself.
That day she went to the library to get some books on growing plants. There were books on vegetable plants, flower plants, trees, pot plants, fruit trees but she didn't even know what kind of plant she had.
Did it matter she thought. After some time in the library she got out five different books on five different topics and went home to read them. She realized after some time that they all had a few things in common. Water, sunshine and fertilizer.

So she got some fertilizer from the shed and sprinkled it on the soil. Then she found a sunny spot to place her plant. Every morning she would give it some water and watch it for a while wondering what sort of plant it would turn out to be.
It took weeks and weeks and the plant grew and grew. Eventually little fruit appeared. Each day when she went out the fruit was a little bigger and a little redder. Then one lovely morning when she went to give it water she was delighted to find bright juicy strawberries all ready to eat. She picked them and raced in to show Aunt Sophy. That night they had strawberries for desert, it was delicious.

The next morning sitting at the bottom of her bed in a basket was a fluffy new puppy.

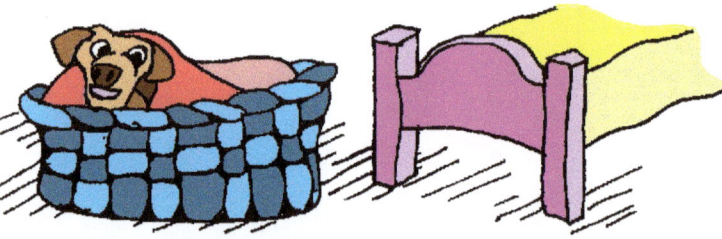

MORAL – You can't have privileges without responsibility.

TRUTHFULNESS

LESSON PLAN

DAY 1

PRAYER: Sing prayers that have been learnt and any others that the children know. Ask them to be reverent because they are talking to God.

STAR BOX: What is in the box? A toy boat (relate it to the story)

STORY: "Truth Floats"

DISCUSSION: What does truthfulness mean?
Being truthful means to always tell things exactly they way things are not not pretend or make up another story.
If we accidentally break something and someone asks who did it how could we be truthful?
Optional - Use discussion points sheet at the beginning of the book to help discuss the meaning of truthfulness.

SONG: "Tell The Truth" - sing with actions

QUOTE:
"Truthfulness is the foundation of all the virtues of the world of humanity."
    'Abdu'l-Bahá
Place the quotation in the letterbox as described in the beginning of the book. These are the messages God has sent us through special people. Ask a child to take out the letter.
Ask the children to say the quotation with you a couple of times. Discuss what it means.

Discussion - How can people respect us if we are not truthful? How can people be our friend if we are not truthful? How can people believe us if we are not truthful? Truthfulness as the bases by which every other quality or virtue in us can develop and grow.

ACTIVITY: Truthfulness Foundations – Use activity sheet on the next page.
Purpose – to understand the quotation – to understand that if we are not truthful our other qualities cannot develop to their full potential.

DAY 2

PRAYER: Sing prayers that have been learnt and any others that the children know. Ask them to be reverent because they are talking to God.

SONG: "Tell The Truth" - sing with actions

DISCUSSION REVIEW: What does truthfulness mean?

GAME: Each person says three foods, two that they do like (truth) and one that they don't (lie). The rest of the group needs to guess which one is the lie.
Purpose – to practice the difference between truth and untruth.

QUOTE VISUALISATION:
"Truthfulness is the foundation of all the virtues of the world of humanity."
    'Abdu'l-Bahá
Photocopy the quote visualisation page. Go through the quote with the children to help them become familiar with the words and understand the meaning. Older children may be able to memorize it. Give each child a copy of the page to colour in. Choose an activity from the front of the book to present the quotations creatively.

EACH CHILD WILL NEED:
- Scissors, glue
- A copy of a house
- Half a piece of A4 coloured card
- Crayons / pencils

TRUTHFULNESS
TRUTHFULNESS FOUNDATIONS

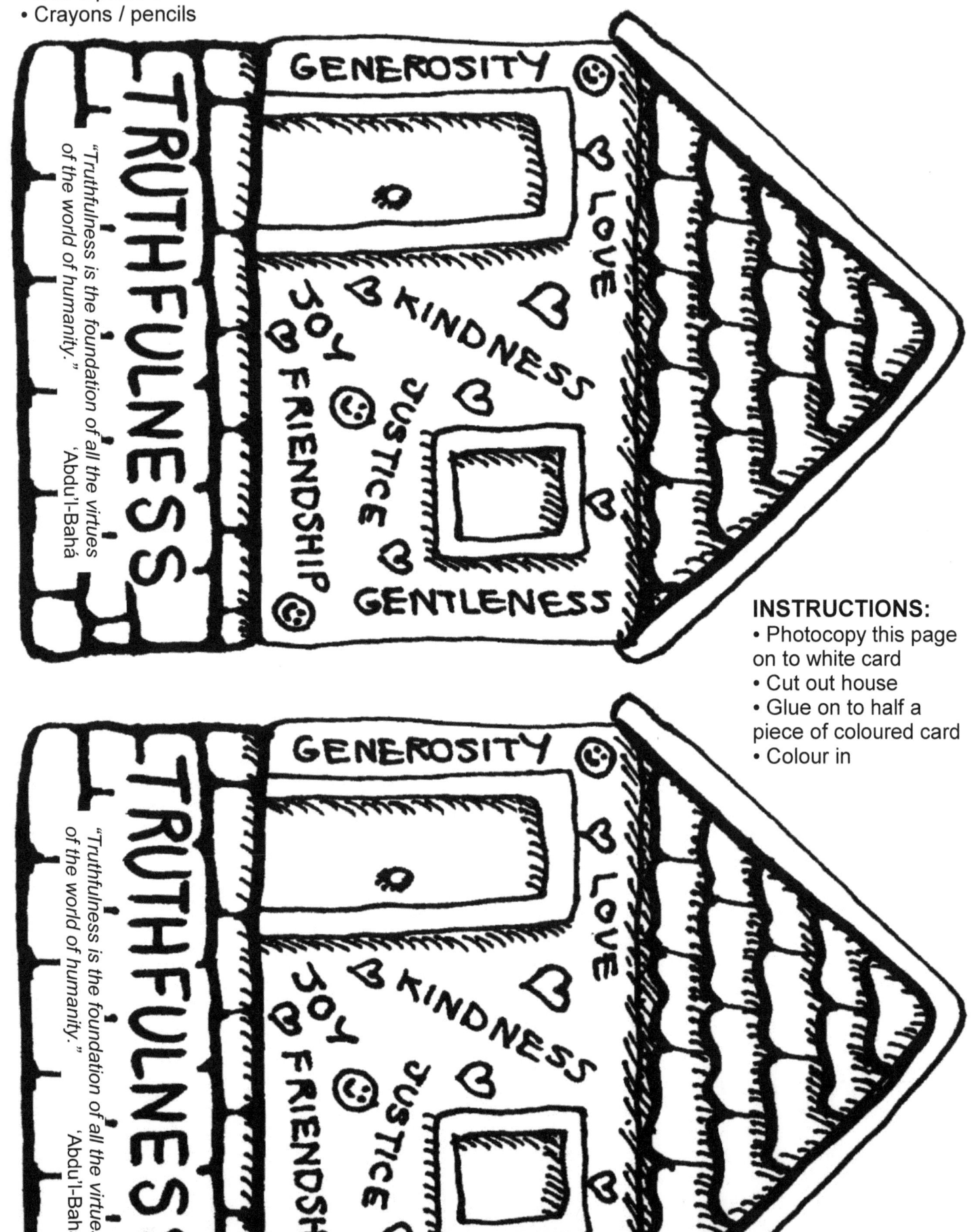

INSTRUCTIONS:
- Photocopy this page on to white card
- Cut out house
- Glue on to half a piece of coloured card
- Colour in

Quote Visualisation

TRUTHFULNESS

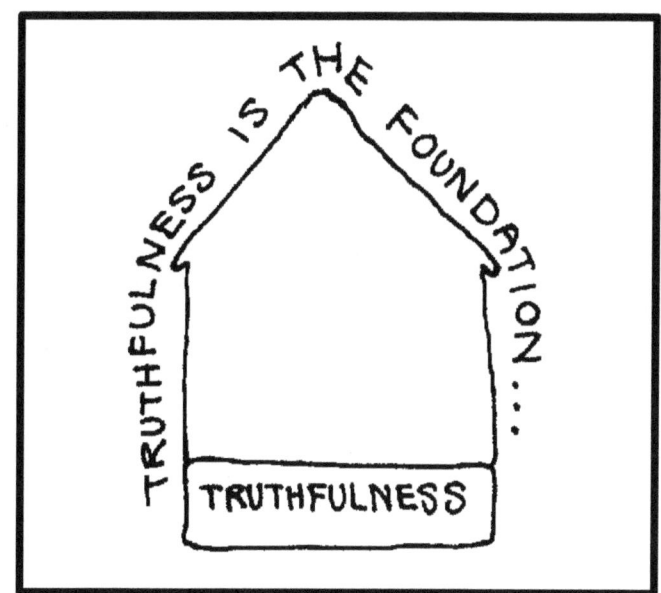
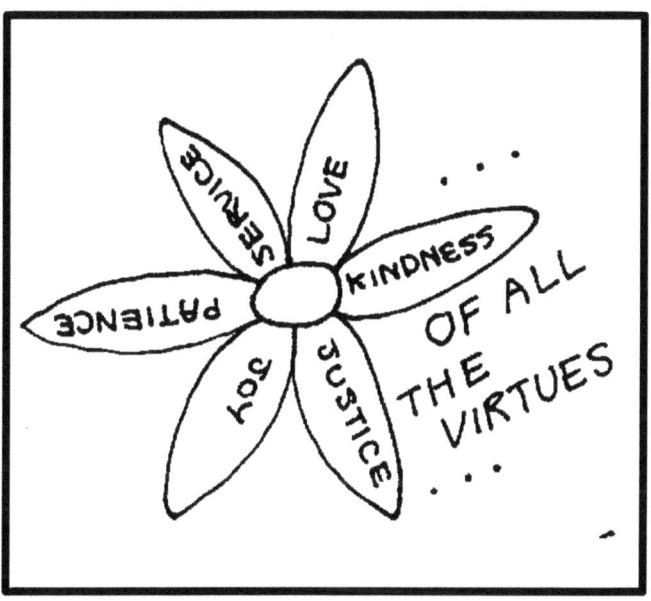

TRUTH FLOATS

TRUTHFULNESS STORY

Ben and Bob were building boats.
"Mine is the best," Bob would boast. "It's has the best colour, the best sail, it is made of the best wood and I am the best builder."
"It's a lovely boat," Ben would reply. "I am not a very good builder."
Ben would ask everyone who wandered past their ideas. He asked them about what the best wood was, what paint would be most water proof, which sail would catch the wind the best. He asked all the experts who worked near the beach.

Bob however, didn't ask anyone anything, he would just keep telling everyone else about how much he knew and how good his boat was going to be.

Finally the day came that both boats were finished. They pushed the boats into the water to test them out. Bob had invited lots of people to see his boat launch. There was quite a crowd by the time they climbed into their boats. Bob was still calling out to the people all the wonderful features of his boat.

They set up their sail and set off. Bob went off as fast as he could waving to his audience. Ben set off slowly, making sure he didn't get anything wrong. Ben could see Bob on the horizon speeding off and then..... "That's funny," thought Ben. Bob's boat seemed to be disappearing. It was sinking, Ben realized. He changed his direction and headed toward the sinking boat. By the time he got there the boat was gone and Bob was left splashing about in the water.

It was a very sad Bob that climbed out and walked up the beach. He confessed sadly to the people waiting there. "I don't really know about boats." The next day Ben helped Bob with another boat. He taught him everything he had learned. This time Bob listened.

MORAL – The truth gets you further in the end, not lies.

EXTRAS

WORDS FOR SONGS
ADDIDIONAL GROUP ACTIVITIES
BADGES

SONGS

GOD

FRUITS OF HUMANITY

Come on, Come on,
and search with me,
for the fruits,
of humanity.

When you find them,
you will be,
kind and loving,
wait and see.

'Abdu'l-Bahá

BE A CANDLE

Gather up the qualities
that make us strong inside.
Make yourself a candle
giving light to far and wide.

Be a candle,
be a candle,
lighting up the world.

Be a candle,
be a candle,
lighting up the world.

Gather up the qualities
that make us strong inside.
Make yourself a candle
giving light to far and wide.

THE Báb

GETTING DRESSED

When I get dressed in the morning,
what do you think I use.
Along with my jumper and pants,
I put on my virtues.

Kindness ties back my hair,
love tucks into my shoes,
respect goes in my pocket,
these are my virtues.

Bahá'u'lláh

IT'S A WIDE WORLD

Put your hands up,
put your hands out,
and clap them both with me.

It's a long world,
it's a wide world,
and wonderful fun to be,

a part of it,
a part of it,
a part of it you see.

a part of it,
a part of it,
a part of it you see.

SONGS

MAIL BOX SONG

There's a message
in the mail box,
what could it be?
It could be something special,
for all of us to see.

There's a message
in the mail box,
what could it be?
It could be something special,
from God,
to you and me.

ORDERLINESS
CLEAN IT UP

Higlety Piglety,
my bedroom,
once was clean,
then went KABOOM.

Higlety Piglety,
use a broom,
clean it up,
my bedroom.

HUMILITY

HUMILITY

Humility is knowing
that you don't know everything,
but you can learn from everyone
and that makes us
somebody special.

When they are big in your eyes,
you are big in their eyes,
so we're all bigger and better.

JOYFULNESS
IN MY HEART

I'm smiling today,
I have a prayer in my heart,
a prayer in my heart,
a prayer in my heart.
I'm smiling today.
I have a prayer in my heart,
a prayer in my heart today.

I'm laughing today,
I have joy in my heart,
joy in my heart,
joy in my heart.
I'm laughing today,
I have joy in my heart,
joy in my heart today.

SONGS

JUSTICE

CROWN OF JEWELS

I have a crown of jewels,
as wonderful as yours.
when I put it on my head,
fairness is my rule.

It's jewels are justice,
justice are its jewels.
It's jewels are justice,
justice are its jewels.

LOVE

LOVE IS A TREASURE

Money disappears as you,
spend it each day.
But love gets only bigger
when you give it away.

Love is a treasure
that only gets bigger
Love is a treasure
you can give away.

CONFIDENCE

I FEEL CONFIDENT

I feel confident with
God right by my side.
Whatever comes my way
I don't feel I need to hide.
Cause I am confident
when God is by my side.

PRAYERFULNESS

GOD WILL BE THERE TOO

Wherever I go, God will be there too.
Wherever I go, God will know his cue.

To cheer me up, help me out
and show me what to do.

Wherever I go, God will be there too.
Wherever I go, God will know his cue.

I pray to him, he answers me
and makes me feel brand new.

Wherever I go, God will be there too.
Wherever I go, God will know his cue.

To cheer me up, help me out
and show me what to do.

SONGS

OBEDIENCE

CAN YOU

Can you all listen,
listen, listen.
Can you all listen,
to everything I say.

Can you all do this,
do this, do this. (action)
Can you all do this,
can you all obey.

RESPECT

RESPECT

I don't understand you,
your very strange to me,
but still I can respect you,
and allow you just to be,

Yourself, the way you are
and the way you want to be.

Although you think I'm different,
confused at what you see,
I know you can respect me,
and allow me just to be,

Myself, the way I am
and the way I want to be.

I don't understand you,
your very strange to me,
but still I can respect you,
and allow you just to be,

Yourself, the way you are
and the way you want to be.

RESPONSIBILITY

I AM RESPONSIBLE

I am responsible,
you just watch me,
I'm ready for a job to do,
just take a look and see.

I won't let you down,
whatever it might be,
because I am responsible,
just take a look and see.

I am responsible,
I am responsible,
I am responsible,
just you look at me.

UNITY

UNITY

When we're on our own we're weak
and what we do is small,
but when we work in unity
we're the strongest of them all.

Unity, Unity,
Unity, Unity,
is the strongest of them all.

SONGS

THOUGHTFULNESS

THE INSIDE

It's the inside that matters,
the outside just gets old.
That's why the inside,
is worth much more than gold.

I can't see it, I can't see it,
but I can feel it, I can feel it,
that's why:

It's the inside that matters,
the outside just gets old.
That's why the inside,
is worth much more than gold.

DETACHMENT

LET GO

Let go, Let go,
just spread your wings.
Fly like the birds,
above all things.

Just soar, soar,
soar like a bird.

Soar, soar,
soar like a bird.

Soar with your spirit,
you don't have wings,
but you can still fly,
above all things.

Just soar, soar,
soar like a bird.

Soar, soar,
soar like a bird.

Let go, Let go,
just spread your wings.
Fly like the birds,
above all things.

TRUTHFULNESS

TELL THE TRUTH

If you tell a lie
then soon no-one
will believe you,
no-one will believe you,
no-one will believe you.

When you tell the truth
people can
rely on you,
can rely on you,
can rely on you.

PERSEVERANCE

DON'T STOP

Round and round the circle goes,
dance about on your toes,
we will not slow or stop,
till we all drop, drop, drop.

Then up we get and round we go,
jumping high and crouching low.
We will not slow or stop,
till we all drop, drop, drop.

SONGS

SERVICE

GIVE AND TAKE

I give to you,
you give to me,
and we all serve happily,
with a give and a take
and a wiggle and a shake,
we all serve happily.

KINDNESS

KINDNESS TIME

Wherever you go,
whoever you meet,
make kindness,
guide your feet.

Step, step, step,
step in time.
Step, step, step,
its kindness time.

COURTESY

COURTESY

Thankyou, please, excuse me,
are the way you share,
your courtesy with others
and show them that you care.

Thankyou, please, excuse me,
are you all aware that,
people will respect you when,
you show them that you care.

PATIENCE

BE PATIENT

All conditions,
all the time.
Happy, sad,
rain or shine.
Be patient,
all the time.

So dry your eyes,
make a smile,
take a breath,
wait a while.

CLEANLINESS

WASH, WASH, WASH

Wash your hands
every day,
Wash, wash, wash,
your o.k.

Scrub your body
every day,
Scrub, scrub, scrub,
your o.k.

Think clean thoughts
every day,
Think, think, think
your o.k.

GROUP FILLER

EXTRA ACTIVITY

INSTRUCTIONS:
• Cut out the top of the tree using Two pieces of large (A1) green card.
• Cut out the trunk of the tree using one piece of large (A1) brown card.
• Cut out fruits using the template on red card.
• Collage the top of the tree using different shades of green paper.
• Collage the trunk of the tree using different shades of brown paper.
• Collage the fruits of the tree using different shades of pink / purple / red paper.
• Type out the quotation in large print and glue it on to the trunk of the tree.
• Glue on the top of the tree and the fruits.
• Type out the virtues and glue one on to each fruit.

NOTE:
• Keep the tree and glue on a new fruit every time you learn about a new virtue.
• This activity can be done at the end of each class to keep the children occupied until the parent picks them up.
• This activity can also be made and used for a presentation at the end of the term with the children singing a related song for the parents.

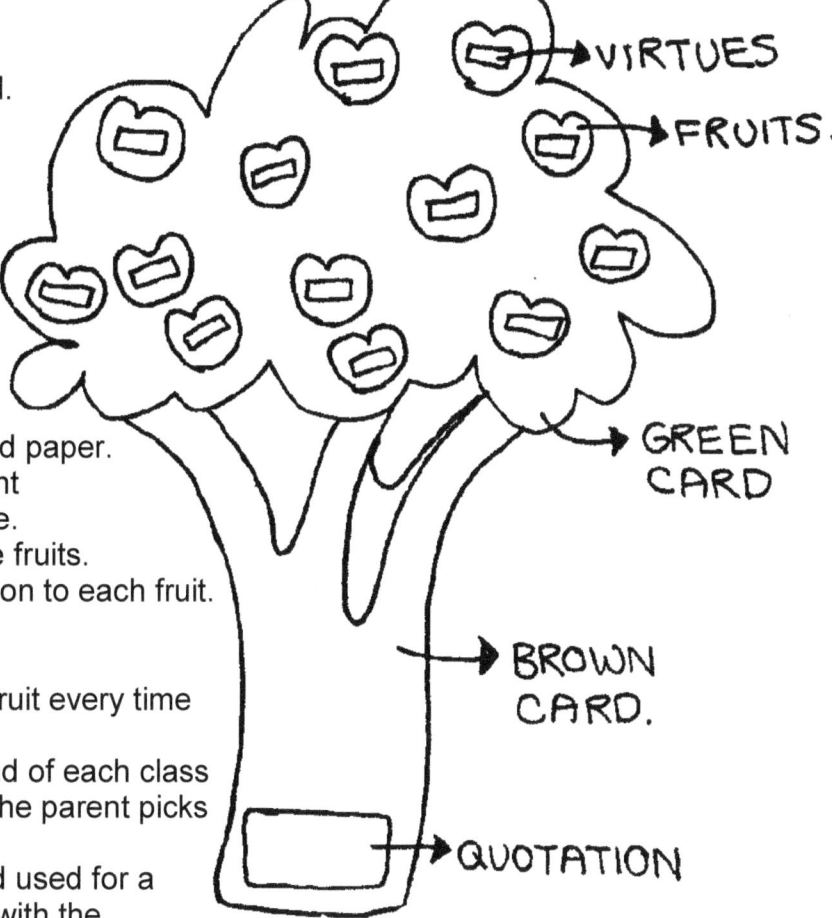

"that... our faults become virtues, our ignorance transformed into knowledge; in order that we might attain the real fruits of humanity..."
'Abdu'l-Bahá

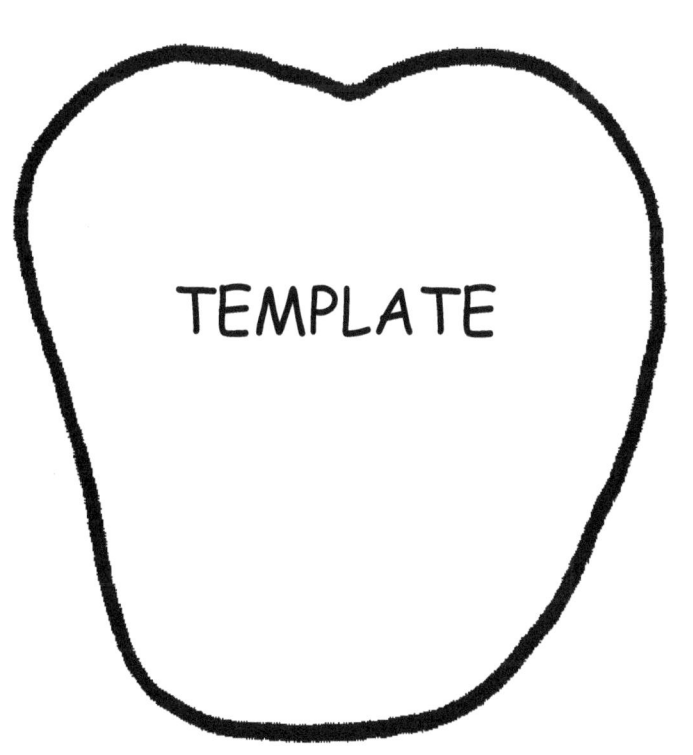

EXTRA ACTIVITY

GROUP FILLER

INSTRUCTIONS:
• Cut out a large heart shape using two A1 sheets of red or pink card.
• Children trace theiir hands on to card.
• Collage the hands with shiny pieces of paper.
• Trim around the edges.
• Glue hand prints on to heart.
• Copy the quotation below and glue into the centre.

NOTE:
• This activity can be done at the end of each class to keep the children occupied until the parent picks them up.
• This activity can also be made and used for a presentation at the end of the term with the children singing a related song for the parents.

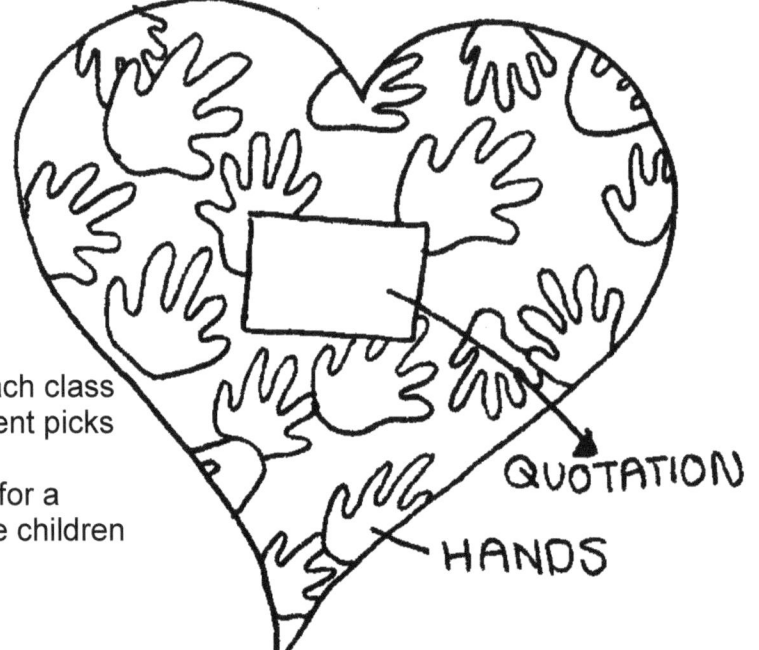

"Take pride not in love for yourselves but in love for your fellow-creatures. Glory not in love for your country, but in love for all mankind."

Bahá'u'lláh

GROUP FILLER

EXTRA ACTIVITY

INSTRUCTIONS:
- Cut a large circle out of two A! Pieces of blue card joined together.
- Cut out red card in the shape of the countries of the world.
- Use a template to cut out people and stick them on to the countries.
- Copy the quotation below and glue onto the circle in an empty space.

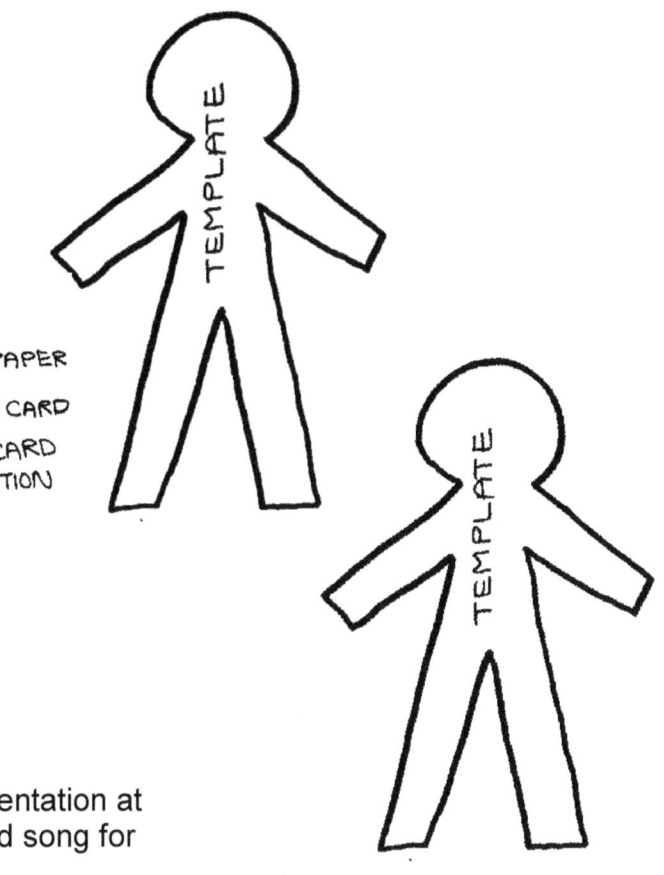

NOTE:
- This activity can be done at the end of each class to keep the children occupied until the parent picks them up.
- This activity can also be made and used for a presentation at the end of the term with the children singing a related song for the parents.

"that... each may become like a lighted candle in the world of humanity."

'Abdu'l-Bahá

EXTRA ACTIVITY

GROUP FILLER

INSTRUCTIONS:
• Cut out a shirt in red A1 card.
• Cut out trousers in Blue A1 card.
• Cut out head, hands, feet in Yellow A1 card.
• Glue person together.
• Print out virtues onto red, blue and brown card.
Cut them out and glue them onto the matching colour of the body. (Hair is brown, shirt is red and trousers are blue).
• Copy the quotation below and glue it into the centre of the shirt.

NOTE:
• This activity can be done at the end of each class to keep the children occupied until the parent picks them up.
• This activity can also be made and used for a presentation at the end of the term with the children singing a related song for the parents.

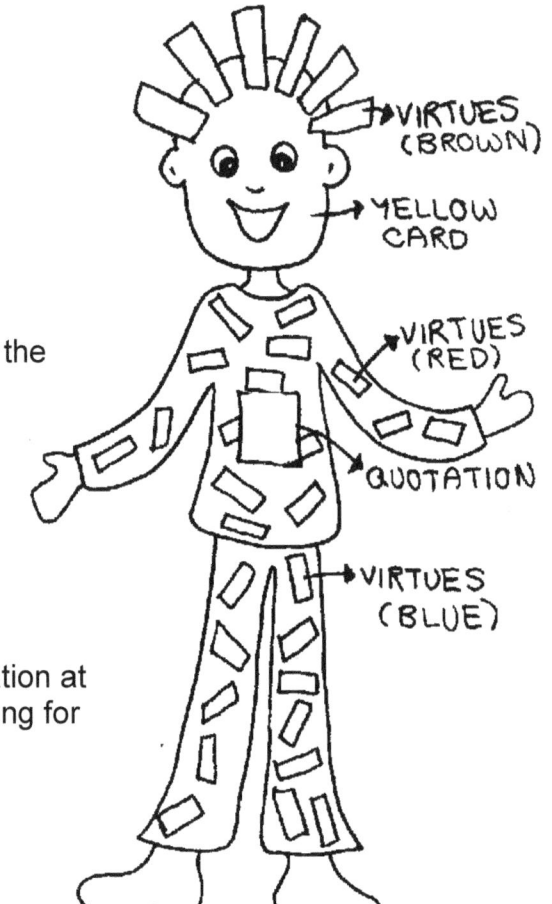

"*Purge your hearts of worldly desires, and let angelic virtues be your adorning.*"

The Báb

STAR BOX PICTURES

PICTURES AS ALTERNATIVES TO OBJECTS

147

BADGES

IDENTIFICATION BADGES

INSTRUCTIONS:
- Copy this sheet on to a coloured piece of card.
- Laminate
- Cut out stars.
- Tape a safety pin on to the back of each star.
- Write in name of teacher or assistant.

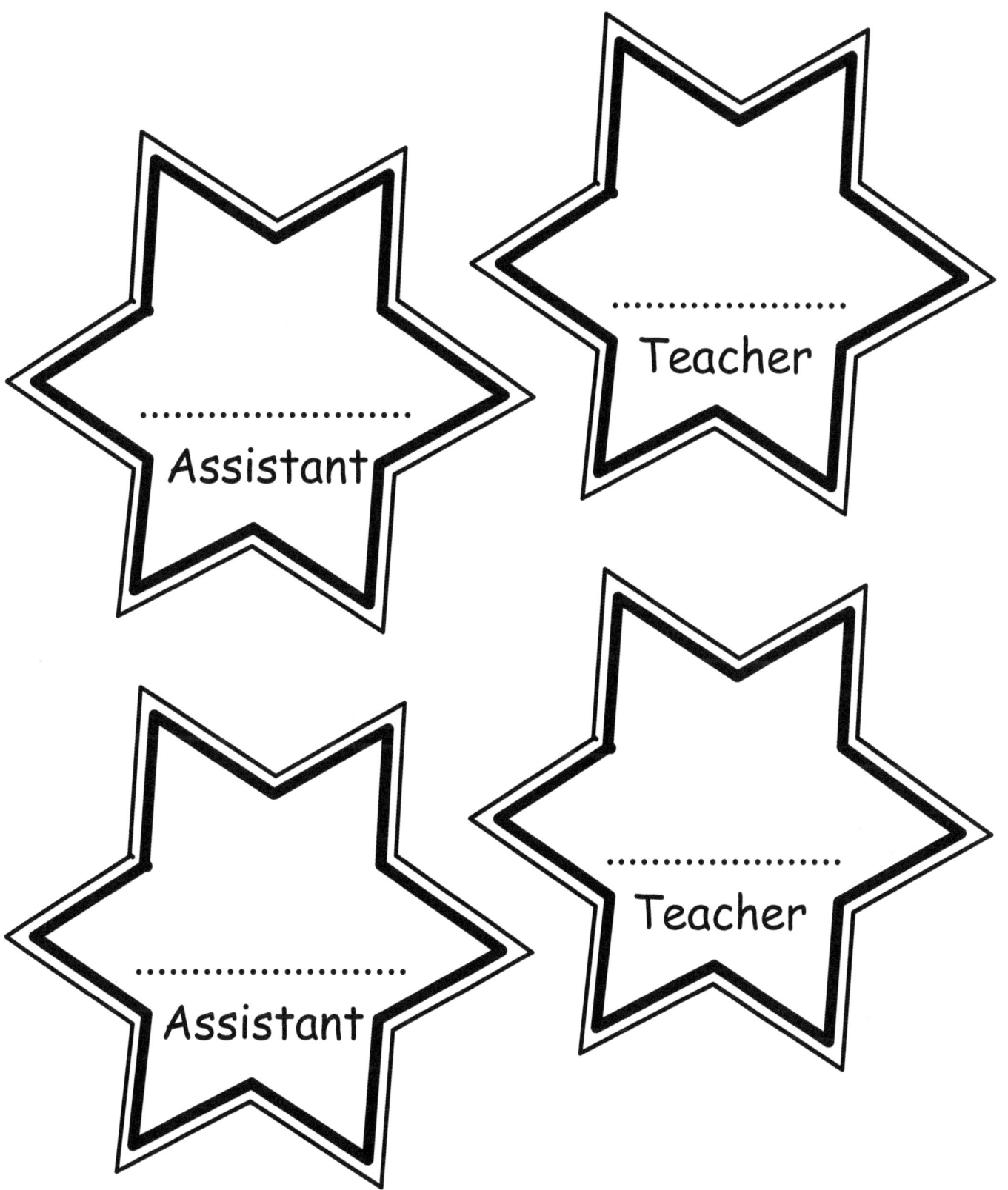

www.ingramcontent.com/pod-product-compliance
Lightning Source LLC
Chambersburg PA
CBHW061055170426
43191CB00022B/2441